Values in the Digital World

Ethics and Practices that Underpin Wellbeing

Dr John Bellavance

Publisher: North South Group

Published in Melbourne, Australia

© Dr Johnn Bellavance 2021

ISBN: 978-0-6452554-0-9

Book cover and Chapter Six Graphics by Emmanuel Darbishire

The Australian Curriculum incorporates a set of general capabilities including digital literacy, personal and social capability and ethical understanding. John Bellavance has written a text that will give teachers and parents insights into how these general capabilities can be developed in an integrated way, moving beyond limited "cyber-safety" programs to proactive moral reflection and action through the adoption of a Digital Moral Framework. It treats digital technologies as much more than passive tools, but as a pervasive aspect of our culture which both shapes our children and young people and is in turn shaped by them. The importance of being able to bring moral values to bear on these interactions cannot be underestimated. This book is imbued with deep empathy with, and understanding of, our emerging generations, drawing on decades of interactions with them in classrooms.

David de Carvalho CEO of the Australian Curriculum, Assessment and Reporting Authority

Good teachers uphold moral purposes of education in their practice. Teachers can come to know how to extend the moral purposes of education in sites of digital learning from this book. Based on an ethics of responsibility for others, this research disrupts the often corporatized and instrumental designs of digital spaces. Bellavance's Digital Moral Framework is a gift to teachers who are seeking to understand the ideological purposes of education in changing times.

Glenn Auld, Senior Lecturer, Deakin University, Victoria, Australia

Dr Bellavance has raised his voice in a unique way to rejuvenate the spirit of moral codes within our preteens and adolescent people. This is a high time where this area should be far more focused than any other. As educators, we are seeing so many behavioural and moral problems in a society because the educational curriculum is solely focusing on an outcome and not on a process. His work seems to resolve the issue to a great extent through his excellent work on cyber-ethics and moral behaviour.

Hena Jawaid - School Counsellor - Minaret College, Victoria, Australia

ABOUT THE AUTHOR

 John Bellavance has worked with NGOs and community organisations to support peace building and wellbeing for 40 years. In the 1980s, he and his wife Anne worked with the African American community to fight crack cocaine. His efforts were recognised by the White House, where President Reagan sent him a letter of appreciation for his efforts to rid America of this social ill. In the early 90s he took this fight against drugs to his home country of Canada, were he was able to bring the issue of illicit drugs as a state campaign issue. As part this work he has studied and written about values education for 30 years. The focus of his PhD thesis was the role of values in human/technological interactions with a particular focus on the role of values in the use of Information Technologies by high school age children. He has been teaching Information Technology in high schools for 20 years in the areas of computer networks, programming and data analytics.

Website: www.drjohn.online

DEDICATIONS

This book is dedicated to my wife Anne and my children who patiently supported me through my many years of study. I am grateful to the school, teachers, parents and students who supported me in my study. I want to thank Dr Glenn Auld for believed in me from the start and throughout of my academic journey. I also want to thank Dr Nicola Johnson and Dr Scott Bulfin who supervised my PhD. Nicola raised me academically to a new standard with much patience and due diligence. Professor Charles Ess read this entire book and provided such valuable insight, and for this, I am grateful. Finally, I want to thank my proof-readers. It is said that it takes a village to raise a child; well it took a loving family and an academic village to raise me as an academic.

Table of Contents

INTRODUCTION

~

A Teacher's Journey

This book tells the story of *Values in the Digital World* that demonstrate the best of human morality and ethics in the use of Information and Communication Technologies (ICTs). Yet, it also tells the story of how ICTs can be used to hurt others without a need to engage with one's own sense of right and wrong, which can lead to a sense of exemption from moral responsibility.

This book is based on my PhD study and my interactions with young people on daily basis in the context of teaching Information and Communication Technologies (ICTs) in high schools, for now 20 years. My study involved interviews with a small group of secondary school students aged 14-15 years old, their parents and teachers. I discussed values in the digital world with some these students and teachers over a period of four years. I wanted to understand adolescent moral development in the context of their use of ICTs. I considered:

1. How do moral reasoning, moral emotion and moral behaviour (the moral domains) mediate secondary school students' uses of Information and Communication Technologies (ICTs)?

2. How to foster the moral values and abilities that mediate the moral domains while using ICTs?

The first outcome of my study is a Digital Moral Framework (DMF) that parents and teachers can use to foster moral values and abilities, and address moral challenges faced by young people while using ICTs. The second outcome is the Cyber Values Systems model (CVS) that can be used to understand the role of values (moral and immoral) in the use of ICTs.

Challenges Faced by Young People

ICTs have been greeted with enthusiasm in education and in society because these provide incredible means for moral action, productivity, innovation and creativity. However, unethical and inappropriate practices are challenging society and educational institutions to understand the moral values and abilities that can mediate the use of ICTs by young people, and help them respond to the challenges they face. The digital cultures in which young people live are reworking the rules by which school, cultural expression and civic life operate. Despite much interest shown by national and state governments with respect to the importance of educating with values, and social and emotional intelligence, we are at a beginning stage with respect to understanding the role of moral values and abilities in the use of ICTs by young people.

As a teacher, I often have conversations with students who encounter challenges in the digital world. Their own attitudes, values and anti-social behaviours, and that of others can be detrimental to their social engagement with others, their wellbeing and their moral development. I have seen many examples of moral agency (making moral judgments and acting on these) on the part of students, but also immoral acts while using ICTs. At times, both practices were evident by the same student. It is my experience, although some students behave inappropriately at times such as malicious attempts to damage the reputation of peers, inappropriate responses and profiles on social media, they also demonstrate moral agency such as standing up to cyberbullies and supporting their peers in need in the digital world. Because young people can be both moral and immoral, as a teacher I concluded that opportunities for learning are rich.

Tensions and Opportunities

So how do we respond to these challenges? There are tensions between enthusiasm for the opportunities provided by ICTs and the desire to restrict youth practices for the sake of protecting their wellbeing. I have seen some parents and teachers approaching unethical practices with the attitude of either 'putting up with it' or responding with a 'knee jerk' reaction to the 'evils' of technology. Media panics tend to construct some youth activity as risky, while ignoring the positive ways teens interact online.

Fixing the Boat while at Sea

The reality is that the use of ICTs is rich with promise and risks, both of which carry moral consequences and personal responsibility. Young people are often navigating the digital world without the values and skills they need to be good digital citizens. We try to help when things go wrong, but this is like fixing the boat while already at sea with bad practices already set. However, we have an opportunity to be proactive and prepare young people before and after they set sail in the digital world. A proactive approach requires fostering moral agency (one's capacity to act morally).

A large body of literature suggests that moral values have an important role in acquiring the skills that underpin digital citizenship. This can serve as a proactive means of fostering morality and as a preventive measure for addressing potential or existing concerns associated with the use of ICTs by young people.

Young People are in the Driver's Seat

When I began teaching ICTs, the way secondary schools attempted to address misuses and risks associated with the use of ICTs was to create policies that 'controlled' young people's use by restricting ICTs through electronic means such as proxies (servers that filter internet content). Currently, with open access to Wi-Fi and the use of personal Wi-Fis in schools, computer-based restrictions can only be achieved in a very limited way. ICTs provide young people with open 24/7 access to any content and expressions, and young people are in the 'driver's seat'. Because young people manage their own uses of ICTs, the individual plays the most significant role in determining practices and this is where the focus should be. This requires fostering moral values that compel self-reflection, critical evaluations of the use of ICTs, self-regulation and moral agency. Tensions between various approaches to cope with unethical uses of ICTs in schools and in society are difficult to resolve unless schools can define the important values and abilities that students need to have while using ICTs and foster these.

Moral experiences and abilities gained in adolescence form the foundation of adult moral character, agency and sense of responsibility toward community and society. Because of this, there is the need to understand how a moral identity is formed in the digital world. Moral identity refers to the degree to which being a moral person is important to an individual's sense of who they are. This is certainly important for me. This is found to motivate prosocial interactions with others.

Digital Natives - Can Students Do this on Their Own?

Since young people generally know more about the new media environments than most adults do, we must be cautious about constructing teens as natural experts of technology, because this assumes that young people naturally know what to do and are able to acquire the abilities to participate ethically and effectively in the digital world on their own. First, this assumes that young people actively reflect on their experiences and can thus articulate what they learn from their participation in the digital world. Second, that they can develop on their own an ethical framework to guide their participation. Cyber-Safety programs are the main proactive intervention directed to youth with respect to their uses of ICTs. However, these programs do not really address the underlying issue of the values that drive problems. Let us begin our journey into values in the digital world by understanding what makes us moral.

CHAPTER ONE

What Makes us Moral Human Beings?

The quest to understand what makes a human being moral is as old as philosophy itself. Currently, moral development, and social and emotional learning with respect to young people is basically conceptualised in two ways. First, children acquire values through both role modelling and socialisation from parents, family members, teachers, peers, and individuals and groups that the child is attached to. Second, because the child is an active interpreter of information, they grow morally through self-reflection by making efforts to become aware of their own values and behaviours, and by trying to change the values and behaviours that they consider inappropriate. Experiences in the digital world can provide young people opportunities to reflect on their values and behaviours.

What are Values?

We need to be able to distinguish between personal, moral and immoral values. Personal values involves our like and dislikes with respect to music, clothing, the arts and so on. Moral values, such as justice have public implications because they affect others. In this sense, a lack of justice or fair treatment of others has implications beyond me personally, hence society sets the importance of moral values in its norms and legal systems.

Conversely, immoral values also impact others in a negative way and are considered contrary to the public good.

Moral Reasoning, Moral Emotion and Moral Behaviour

What makes us moral incorporates aspects of the cognitive (reasoning), affective (emotions) and behavioural domains (the moral domains) of psychological functioning and development. To understand morality we must account for how these moral domains connect and interact with each other to form the moral person.

To investigate the role of values and the moral domains in the use of ICTs, I reviewed the literature on moral and developmental psychology, computer ethics, new media and the Australian and Victorian curriculum frameworks. The Australian Curriculum and the Victorian Curriculum were also included because these reflect guidelines that schools in Australia need to consider when planning teaching and learning with respect to emotional and social abilities. I suspect that similar guidelines exist throughout the world.

To determine which values underpin each moral domain, I drew on how moral psychology associates particular values to moral reasoning, moral emotion and moral behaviour. Even though the moral domains are reviewed separately in this book to facilitate understanding, and teaching and learning, the moral domains are inseparably linked. For example, moral emotions are strongly shaped by prior deliberative moral reasoning, while moral emotions influence behaviour. Additionally, the values that the literature indicates are associated with a particular moral domain could arguably underpin other domains. For example, being a person of integrity involves reasoning (having expectations of oneself) and behaving accordingly, hence, the link between reasoning and behaviour. The links between the moral domains are important because they point to a need to take a holistic approach that incorporates all three moral domains when seeking to foster morality.

Let us now take a brief look at how moral development has been understood. The values that are important for each domain are discussed first, followed by abilities associated with moral reasoning, emotion and behaviour.

Moral Psychology and Values

Proposing moral values is not generally considered the role of psychology. However, values are impossible to eliminate from moral psychology because any analysis of moral development must go beyond a descriptive account of what is. It cannot avoid evaluative questions to understand what contributes to positive morality in order to encourage it.

Evolutionary science and research in human behaviour have yielded a consensus that justice, empathy and altruism are part of the biological makeup of our species (Colby & Damon, 2015). Empathy, compassion and conscientiousness (relating to a person's conscience and remorse) are values, but also moral emotions. Altruism and justice are associated with moral behaviours towards others and social responsibility. A personal sense of responsibility and self-control are also considered important for self-management with regard to moral behaviour, while honesty, integrity and authenticity are associated with moral reasoning.

Computer Ethics and Values

Acquiring and understanding the moral values that underpin moral reasoning and behaviour are crucial for computer ethics. Moral reasoning also relies on learning to apply moral values to make moral judgements with regard to ICTs and justifying moral judgements and decisions.

A review of computer ethics suggests that certain values are particularly important with respect to the use of ICTs by young people – authenticity, integrity, honesty, trust, privacy, accountability and responsibility, stand out. Authenticity is being who we truly are regardless of the contexts in which we find ourselves, including while using of ICTs. Being authentic involves us having integrity, being honest and accountable. Having moral integrity also involves having high moral expectation, feeling a sense of personal responsibility and accountability and living up to one's moral values. ICTs are now commonly used by adolescents to construct online public profiles. The construction of these profiles raises issues of the authenticity and honesty because this involves a desire on their part to be validated by their peers and profiles can be more easily manipulated using ICTs.

Another important value and moral concern is privacy and how young people portray themselves. Research has found that the need for popularity was a predictor of whether adolescents posted sexual images of themselves online. Conversely, they were less likely to post sexual images if they had a lower need for popularity (Baumgartner, Sumter, Peter, & Valkenburg, 2015).

Accountability and responsibility are also important because of the virtual nature ("I am not physically there") of the actions taken while using ICTs. ICTs often provide anonymity for the actions of individuals, leaving them to feel less accountable for their actions. Research suggests that anonymity fosters attitudes towards cyberbullying in young people, which also predict subsequent cyberbullying behaviours (Barlett, 2017).

Now let us explore how the moral domains operate with respect to these values.

Moral Reasoning

Initial psychological investigations into moral development were dominated by the role of moral reasoning as the basis for moral development and behaviour. More recently, scholars have questioned whether moral reasoning necessarily results in an actual moral behaviour. It is argued that moral motives are driven in large part by emotions that arise quickly and automatically, and then influenced by moral reasoning, which can correct and override emotions. Reasoning is still important, because the manifestation of moral emotions in adolescents is an indicator that moral values have been internalised (Krettenauer & Malti, 2013). In the course of development, conscious reflection fosters moral understanding, which influences emotional responses. Skilled moral emotions depend on moral reasoning.

Reasoning Abilities

Moral reasoning abilities involve using moral values to evaluate and produce moral arguments, and make decisions. Moral reasoning is important for the early development of moral action tendencies. For example, disengagement from moral reasoning plays a role in the continuation of cyberbullying (Perren & Gutzwiller-Helfenfinger, 2012; Wang, Yang, Yang, Wang, & Le, 2017).

Australian and Victorian Curriculums and the Moral Domains

The Australian Curriculum suggests that self-awareness and self-reflection are important reasoning skills. Identifying and describing factors that influence a student's emotional responses are important for self-awareness. With respect to moral behaviour, self-management involves behavioural skills such as, self-discipline and the ability to delay gratification. Moral behaviour also requires social awareness of others. This includes altruism (assisting others), a sense of justice, in the form of analysing discrimination (racism and sexism), showing respect for others' perspectives, emotional states and needs, and responsibility towards others. Fostering behavioural skills involves students identifying strategies to manage themselves in a range of situations.

Self-awareness and understanding others are also considered important by the Victorian Curriculum. Moral reasoning abilities involve evaluating and finding resolutions to ethical problems and understanding the ethical principles that are common across people and cultures. Students need to investigate fairness, equality, respect and tolerance. To foster these skills, it is recommended that students explore a range of ethical problems and examine the extent to which different positions share common ethical principles. Students are also required to explore how they manage their reasoning, emotions and experiences.

Moral Emotion

Moral psychology shows that experiencing appropriate emotions and managing them well is essential for morality. Moral emotions are self-evaluative (conscience and remorse) and other-oriented emotions (empathy). They also support motivation for actions, self-regulation and developing relations with others.

Empathy

Empathy is linked to the ability to coordinate perspectives of self and others in children, while deficiencies in empathy are predictors of adolescents' antisocial behaviours. Adolescents engaging in cyberbullying tend to score lower in empathy measures (Lazuras, Barkoukis, Ourda, & Tsorbatzoudis, 2013). The more empathetic people are, the more they are willing to follow moral values. Individuals with more developed emotional intelligence are better able to discern the morally relevant factors of a situation (Cameron & Payne, 2013; Goleman, 2004; Schalkwijk, Stams, Stegge, Dekker, & Peen, 2016).

Empathy facilitates social interactions, nurture relationships, acts as a protective factor that promotes young people's psychosocial adjustment and helps individuals to overcome risk factors such as aggression and immoral behaviours. A study of teenagers' online experiences indicates that they encounter situations that cause them to feel anger (Greenfield, 2008), suggesting the need for empathy. The level of empathy felt by the individual is associated with more lenient moral judgments of others and tempers anger with compassion in situations where activities cause frustration and anger (Cameron & Payne, 2013; Giner-Sorolla, 2012; Goleman, 2004).

Abilities associated with empathy include understanding and feeling what another person is experiencing and feeling, being more forgiving, recognising that moral transgressions have negative consequences on others, acting out of concern for the wellbeing of others and seeking to alleviate the suffering of others.

The Conscience

Conscientiousness is defined by some moral psychologists as a person's integrated moral values which act as internal moral sanctions that guide decision making and behaviour (the voice of the conscience) (Berkowitz & Grych, 1998; Juthberg & Sundin, 2010; Schalkwijk et al., 2016). The conscience influences behaviour in two ways. First, it leads to self-evaluations as a result of emotional discomfort (remorse) following a behaviour that is in opposition to one's own moral values. Second, it influences moral reasoning when evaluating behavioural intentions. In this respect, it fosters moral responsibility and acts as a deterrent for immoral behaviour.

Abilities associated with conscience involves reasoning about one's actions and the emotional experience of feeling committed to and accountable for one's own moral values, which are closely related to integrity. The conscience is also linked to behaviours that seek to fix what one has done wrong, such as apologising for misbehaviours.

Moral Behaviour

There are two dimensions to moral behaviour: self-management and social responsibility towards others. Abilities associated with self-management include self-awareness, being honest with oneself and self-control. Behavioural psychology has demonstrated that self-control plays a significant role in self-management in academic, occupational and social success (Ent, Baumeister, & Tice, 2015; Schalkwijk et al., 2016). Conversely, low self-control is a significant risk factor for a broad range of personal and interpersonal problems. Values and abilities associated with social responsibility include altruism, justice and respect. Let us now investigate how to foster morality.

Moral Psychology and Fostering the Moral Domains

Moral reasoning is fostered in part, by the acquisition of moral values. Moral reasoning provides a means for values to become part of the individual's moral identity. Teaching children how to identify the moral aspects of a situation is important because reasoning about right and wrong is necessary to take the perspective of another. Providing opportunities for youth dialogue is one suggested means of acquiring this moral reasoning skill, as groups and collaborative thinking play an essential role in moral change. Practical wisdom is acquired through children's active participation in relationships with adults, peers, cultural practices and social institutions. A study of cyberbullying among teenagers concluded that moral training targeting maladaptive normative beliefs can form the basis for educational programs and preventive strategies (Lazuras et al., 2013). Fostering the link between moral reasoning (duties) and the consequences of behaviours also needs to occur.

Empathy can be taught effectively through school-based programs, first because moral emotions partly rely on the acquisition of moral values and second, because narratives that appeal to emotions foster moral learning. Empathy also builds on self-awareness, as the individual learns to distinguish between the perspectives of the self and others. The conscience is fostered when people come to recognise that moral transgressions have a negative impact on others and learn from their mistakes.

Parental involvement and connection with the adolescent foster moral reasoning and behaviour. Modelling moral values in the life of the child is another important means of fostering morality, as are peer groups, which can serve to positively reinforce and influence behaviour.

CHAPTER TWO

Do we Drive Technology or Does Technology Drive us?

Young people need to understand how their values and behaviours affect their activities and others in the digital world, but also how the
digital world affects their values and behaviours. This understanding will help shape their good practices as participants in online communities. As we navigate the digital world, it is a two-sided story of the reciprocal

effect of humans on the digital world and the digital world on humans. The Cyber Values Systems (CVS) model presented in this chapter is used to understand such effects, but also provides guidance with respect to values in the digital world.

As we investigate the immoral values that mediate the use of ICTs, this highlights the importance of the need for particular moral values and behaviours. Having said this, we should not to adopt a reactive or deficit approach by mostly focusing on the detrimental effects of ICTs on morality. This view can result in a restricting the benefits ICTs can offer. A second problem of focusing on the detrimental features of ICTs can result in downplaying the significance of the moral agency that young people have while using ICTs. For this reason, the CVS model is also used in the next chapter to show the moral reasoning, emotions and behaviours (moral agency) that young people engage in while using ICTs.

To understand how the digital world affects the values and behaviours of young people we need to critically evaluate the morally relevant properties and practices that make up the digital world. Such an investigation is necessary to understand the less visible implications of the ICTs on morality and its influences on human welfare. We need to make transparent the moral features of practices and technologies that would otherwise remain hidden, thus making them available for ethical analysis and moral decision-making. This provides an understanding of the influences that can potentially support or undermine the moral domains of young people while using ICTs. With this understanding, we can anticipate difficulties, identify opportunities, take a proactive approach to fostering values and resolve problems related to the use of ICTs.

In the first section of this chapter we explores sociotechnical conceptualisations, namely how we perceive the use and effects of ICTs on values and social life. The second section discusses systems theory because this can be used for analysing and modelling interactions between the social sphere and technology. The third section briefly outlines the Cyber Values Systems (CVS) model which specifically shows the role of values in sociotechnical phenomena. In the fourth section the CVS model is used to understand Technologically Mediated Moral Issues, namely how values impact and are impacted while using ICTs.

Sociotechnical Conceptualisations

How we view the use and effects of ICTs on values and social life influences the judgements we make about the moral implications of ICTs, how we implement these, and the policies and the teaching and learning approaches used to guide and transform their use. These views/conceptualisations are relevant for understanding young people's values and practices, and the influence of ICTs on their values. Questions and concerns are still currently being investigated and contested when it comes to the use of ICTs by adolescents. For example, whether ICTs cause social change or are an outcome of social change, or both. So how do we view our impact on technology and its impact on us (sociotechnical views)? There are three basic views – the instrumental, substantive and 'third position'.

Just a Tool

The instrumental paradigm posits that technologies are neutral tools and values free; they are a means to an end established by humans. Technology is subservient to the human values and moral concerns only arise when humans use technologies immorally. The instrumental paradigm mainly views the implementation of technology through valuing effectiveness, strategic control and economic utility, which is the dominant view adopted by modern governments and policy sciences. This is a view now completely rejected in philosophy of technology and related fields.

The substantive paradigm, views technologies has being shaped by the interests of the people who produce and control them, and these 'interests' are embedded in the design, deployment and uses of technologies. No tool is neutral because technologies have inbuilt interests that affect the social dimension.

These two views present us with a limited perspective. We cannot consider the influences of the social sphere and technology in isolation, because the influence of both the social sphere and technology need to be considered for our understanding to be comprehensive.

The 'third position' incorporates the reciprocal impact of humans and technology on each other. First, humans affect ICT environments (the digital world) through the values, goals and behaviours they bring. ICT environments are systems that are made up of people and digital technologies. Second, values, goals and techniques such as computer codes are added to ICTs environments, which affect the social sphere. Third, the reciprocal influence of the social sphere on ICTs and the influence of ICTs on the social sphere need to be considered. Interactions that are accounted for in context provide a more holistic view of sociotechnical phenomena. This is the position taken in this book.

Systems Theory - A Holistic Approach to Modelling Sociotechnical Phenomena

The whole is greater than the sum of its parts - Aristotle

I used systems theory to create the Cyber Values Systems (CVS) model to understand the role of values in the use of ICTs by young people. Systems theory-modelling principles are widely used to understand the complexity of the world, analyse problems and find solutions. The basic idea is that the system as a whole determines in an important way how the parts behave - the whole is greater than the sum of its parts. This is also true for sociotechnical phenomena. A systems approach is an alternative to reductionist approach, which seeks to understand an individual system (a young person) or parts, by examining them in isolation from other parts or systems (social media). Systems theory relies on several components for modelling. In this chapter, we seek to understand information processing, adaptation to change, self-organisation and goal-directed behaviours with respect to human values in the use of ICTs.

The first components are the systems. For example, the two systems can be young person and their interactions with social media (ICT environments). The processes that need to be understood are the reciprocal influences of the values of a young person acts on (outputs) while using social media, and the values and actions that occur on social media (inputs) that affect a young person's values and behaviours (see Figure 2.1).

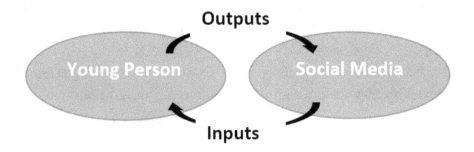

Figure 2. 1 – Two Systems Interacting

Circularity and Feedback

Circularity is the process in which an effect feeds back onto its very cause, a process that is found in all complex systems, organisms and social structures. When a young person (a system) interacts with social media - events and positive feedback (inputs) that occur in that ICT environment affect the person, to which they seek to respond. Outputs (negative feedback) are the impacts the young person (also a system) has on the ICT environment. In its simplest form, the behaviours of a system are outputs that result from inputs from its environment.

Goals, Communication and Control

Another process is goal directed behaviour. When individuals act in their environment they choose their values and goals. For human systems, the preferred goals are values and objectives that humans adhere to and allow them to maintain their preferred state. They make decisions based on what they observe (the disturbances in the environment), how this affects their goals and values, and then act based on these processes (see Figure 2.2).

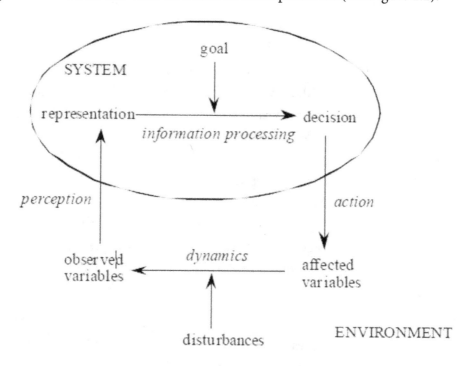

Figure 2.1 The basic components of a control system - (Heylighen, Joslyn, & Turchin, 1999)

Cyber Values Systems (CVS) Model

Systems theory modelling principles described above were used to create the Cyber Values System (CVS) which models the role of moral and immoral values while using ICTs. A more detailed analysis using real life experiences of the reciprocal moral and immoral influences of humans and the digital world (ICTs) on each other is undertaken in the next chapter.

Using the CVS model, the role of values can be understood based on the following three processes, which can influence the moral reasoning, emotions and behaviours of young people (see Figure 2.3 below):

1. In the first process, outputs - human values, goals and techniques (moral and immoral) affect the use of ICTs by individuals and their deployment by organisations. When individuals act in ICT environments, they do so based on their preferred goals and values. Negative feedback are the values and goals held by the individual, which form the basis of the judgements and decisions they make with respect to what is occurring in ICT environments. This also involves their desire to control and maintain their preferred values in that environment. A human observes the inputs (values and events) in the ICT environment. This perception creates a representation (a model) of what is happening in the ICT environment. The information is processed to determine in what way these values and events affect the values and goals of the human system, and the best way to safeguard the preferred values of the human system. Based on this information, the human system makes a decision on what actions need to be taken and the action is taken (output).

Why is this important? Ethical decision making of young adults demonstrates that personally held values are the most important factors for determining moral or immoral behaviours while using ICTs (Yoon, 2011). Conversely, immoral values such as: a lack of integrity, deception, violations of trust, defamation, disinformation, intellectual property violations, privacy violations, cyberbullying and abuses of power also influence ICT environments.

2. In the second process, values and events (inputs) that occur in ICT environments influence human values and social conditions. Inputs are values, goals and techniques that are part of, and coming from, ICT

environments. Humans seek to manage these inputs, which is the process of self-maintenance and goal-directed behaviour. An action is taken (negative feedback) by a human system that seeks to affect some part of the ICT environment (the other system). Positive feedback is when inputs coming from ICT environments cause human values (a system) to change, which can lead to an increase in a behaviour.

3. The third process involves circularity - the reciprocal moral and immoral influence of humans and ICTs on each other. Circularity is a process where an effect feeds back onto its very cause. Because of circularity, outputs from human systems into ICT environments feedback to human systems in the form of inputs coming from ICT environments.

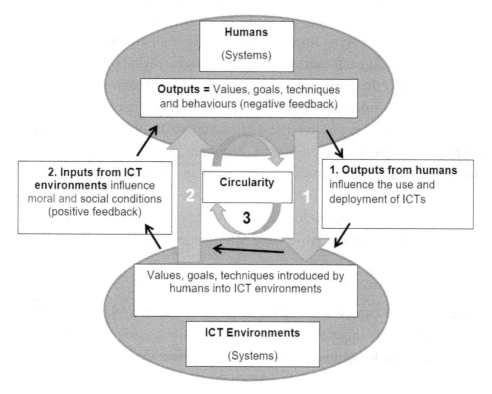

Figure 2.3 – The Cyber Values Systems (CVS) model

The Influence of Human Values on ICT Environments

Computer ethicists generally agree that the values held by individuals affect moral reasoning (Blau & Eshet-Alkalai, 2017; Mercier, 2011; Yoon, 2011) and moral behaviour (Ess, 2002; Floridi, 1999) while using ICTs. Young people are experimenting with and creating new social identities through the use of ICTs. It is important to understand how their values influence these online social identities and wellbeing.

Digital Images and Digital Shadows

Self-definition is important since it is through this process that adolescents arrive at their sense of identity, which is often dependent on the perspective and the judgements of others. It is therefore important to understand the moral and wellbeing implications of these online profiles, sometimes referred to as a digital footprint, which is a person's digital traces left behind as they conduct their lives online. Managing these profiles well is considered important for protecting one's reputation and employment prospects. To differentiate between positive and detrimental online public profiles, I refer to positive online public profiles as *digital images* and detrimental online public profiles as *digital shadows*. The moral and wellbeing concern is that the broad reach of young peoples' actions while using ICTs can lead to the creation of digital shadows for themselves and others. This raises concerns for their dignity, privacy, self-esteem and mental wellbeing.

Inauthenticity

Online profiles can be both authentic and inauthentic. While using ICTs individuals can manipulate information about themselves and others more easily, this can be good and bad online profiles. The creation of digital images by adolescents involves a desire on their part to show the positive side of themselves to others; nothing wrong there. This can also be motivated by being validated by their peers and to meet the expectations of others. However, this can lead to problems. First, this can lead to inappropriate postings about themselves and others. Second, enactments of inauthentic digital images can affect a young person's psychological wellbeing by making some individuals feel alienated from their true self because of a lack of authenticity between their online and offline selves (Lim, Nicholson, Yang, & Kim, 2015). Third, the creation of inauthentic digital images can become detrimental digital shadows, which may affect their wellbeing.

The Influence of the Digital World (ICT Environments) on Human Values

In the second process, inputs (positive feedback) are the moral and immoral values, goals and techniques that are part of ICT environments, which influence human values and behaviours, and social conditions. Human systems seek to manage and respond to these inputs (negative feedback). The influence of the values, goals and techniques that are embedded into ICTs by organisations need to be considered because these may be having a moral impact on young people. Probing and exploring these embedded values and revealing their articulations in technology is a vital part of ethical analysis (Ess & Thorseth, 2010).

These influences can be both detrimental and beneficial. With respect to beneficial social effects, ICTs provide more diverse opportunities for self-expression. For some, using ICTs to communicate reduces anxiety and allows for them to express themselves more freely. Additionally, the creation of positive digital images can provide young people with opportunities for self-reflection and opportunities to get positive feedback from peers. For example, young people can reflect about their values when gaming or on social media which can lead to moral learning.

Digital Moral Malleability

There are also detrimental impacts if ICTs on morality. Specific characteristics of ICTs such as anonymity, instrumentality, distance, displacement and the dampening of social-emotional cues, which I refer to as Digital Moral Malleability (DMM), are characteristics of ICTs that can minimise the sense of the consequences of one's actions on others. These characteristics allow us to "bend our morals", as one student put it. The psychological distance that exists between people while using ICTs (the virtual reality) can lead to a sense that actions are not real. ICTs provide an experiential space that is not represented as objectively graspable, but nevertheless bring about effects in reality. The virtual and logically malleable characteristics of ICTs may influence young people to view their actions in the digital world as less real, hence, influencing moral disengagement and increasing anti-social behaviour. This may affect their sense of moral responsibility and accountability and truthfulness.

Digital Shadows - The loss of Autonomy and Self-Image

Young people regularly replicate and spread content widely about others in the digital world. This can be good or bad. Detrimental content posted online by ourselves and others can become a digital shadow that present us in a bad light and effects our wellbeing. Autonomy in the digital age requires a measure of control of one's online profile. The loss of control of one's information and profile is a moral issue because this is a violation of human autonomy, privacy, personal integrity because this undermines our identity, dignity, justice and control. This is important for people because control of their profiles is essential for the formation of their self-definition or sense of identity. Therefore, actions taken by peers in ICT environments may have an impact on the autonomy and self-image of young people. Digital shadows created by others can also lead to a loss of moral autonomy. The creation of a moral identity (the sense of being a moral person) is important for adolescent concept of self and identity. Moral autonomy is defined as owning one's moral voice and the capacity to shape our moral story. When others interfere with this autonomy online this can affect our self-esteem, and can even lead to anger and conflict.

Persistence and Scalability of ICTs

The persistence, replicability, search-ability and scalability of content posted online, exacerbates the problems associated with digital shadows created by ourselves and others. With ICTs, the undermining of our sense of identity is exacerbated by broad public exposure, ubiquitous computing and ungovernable diffusion of information. Once information has been propagated through the use of ICTs, it is difficult to eliminate or even modify. We lose control of our information. Just think about fake news.

The Impact of Digital Moral Malleability on Authenticity

In the previous section, human values are discussed as a driving factor behind inauthentic digital images. This section explores the influence of digital moral malleability on how individuals portray themselves. ICTs dispose individuals to present information in a skewed way to fit their objectives; hence, ICTs can influence the creation of false self-representations. Distance from the audience while using ICTs may also influence how one represents oneself (Barque-Duran, Pothos, Hampton, & Yearsley, 2017).

The Impact of Digital Moral Malleability on Moral Responsibility

Anonymity is characteristic of ICTs, which allows us to act without being identified, providing anonymity for actions. This can influence moral disengagement and lead to anti-social behaviour. Studies have shown that cyberbullies consider anonymity to be desirable because it allows them to feel less inhibited and less accountable for their actions (Christie & Dill, 2016; Price & Dalgleish, 2010). All of this suggests that anonymity may influence the moral reasoning and behaviour of young people.

Digital Moral Malleability - Distance and Victimless Crimes

Another potential influence of digital moral malleability on moral responsibility is the distancing of one's actions from their effects on others. Some computer ethicists have speculated that the remote, immaterial (virtual) and faceless nature of interactions while using ICTs causes individuals to perceive their actions as less 'real', hence distancing individuals from their actions (Floridi, 1999; Nissenbaum, 1994; Runions & Bak, 2015; Wong, 1995). Moral disengagement may occur because of the distance from the victim and the inability to see the victim's reaction. This distance may create an illusion that no harm is done because the aggressor does not have to physically see the direct effect of their harm on the victim. Immoral actions while using ICTs can easily be perceived as 'victimless crimes' (Bartlett & Prica, 2017; Sikka, 2012).

Digital Moral Malleability - Emotional Disengagement

This disburdening effect of ICTs relieves us of the need for emotional engagements with the world, and may also result in individuals having no knowledge of potential harm, because the link between cause and effect is blurred. Dehumanising the target, acts to reframe the individual's perceptions about the target's role, and it is speculated that the invisibility of the victim and the physical distance afforded by ICT communication creates an emotional gap that enables cyberbullies to disregard the emotional consequences of aggressive acts (Perren & Gutzwiller-Helfenfinger, 2012; Runions & Bak, 2015). Another issue associated with distancing, is the absence of nonverbal cues, such as facial expressions and tone of voice (Allison & Bussey, 2017). Removing these cues eliminates one of the conditions for the elicitation of empathy.

Digital Moral Malleability – A Means to an End

ICTs have become synonymous with society's view of modernisation and progress, and as cost-efficient ways to solve a multitude of problems - tools that allow us to achieve what we want. Some computer ethicists have speculated that the instrumental mindset (ICTs are tools to be used as efficiently and effectively as possible) may undermine a sense of moral responsibility and restrict moral evaluations of the potential harm ICTs may cause (Floridi, 1999; Gotterbarn, 1992). This mindset can lead to using technology without considering the moral implications, and opens up the possibility of their exploitation for self-interest and unethical behaviours. The moral ramifications of the instrumental mindset may be that individuals may perceive ICTs as simply a means to an end and view other human beings as a means to their own ends in these technological processes (Ess, 2002). For example, we may consider it wrong to steal chocolate from a shop, but feel differently about stealing and spreading information without permission. Instrumentality may be an attitude adopted by young people because they may view ICTs as tools for their use and enjoyment, which may lead to unethical behaviours.

The Reciprocal Influence of Humans and the Digital World on Each Other

The third process involves circularity - the reciprocal moral and immoral influence of humans and ICTs on each other, which may influence the moral reasoning, emotions and behaviours of young people. Circularity is a process where an effect feeds back onto its very cause. *Outputs* coming from human systems into ICT environments feedback to humans in the form of *inputs* coming from ICT environments – what goes around, comes around. What we put out there, comes back to us. For example, players bring their own values to the gaming experience and online this may feed back to them when others players respond to their values and actions. Players are not passive amoral creatures; they reflect, relate, and create with ethical or unethical minds. The games they play are also ethical systems, with rules that create gameworlds with values at play (Sicart, 2009).

Circularity can reinforce both positive and detrimental behaviours. For example, the creation of positive digital images or positive behaviours online by young people can provide them with opportunities for self-reflection as they get positive feedback from peers, reinforcing positive behaviours. A detrimental impact of circularity is when anonymous actions while using ICTs minimise the immoral consequences of actions on others, and reinforces moral disengagement and anti-social behaviours.

Positive Feedback and Inauthenticity

The ease of information manipulation afforded by ICTs in the creation of inauthentic online profiles may be reinforcing such behaviours. Young people are motivated to present themselves well on social media (outputs). Characteristics of ICTs (inputs) allow them to present inauthentic profiles. Positive feedback from their peers on social media (inputs) may increase the likelihood of them continuing to present inauthentic profiles. The need for popularity may also drive inappropriate behaviours (outputs), which can be reinforced by others on social media (inputs).

Circularity and Instrumentality

Instrumentality could also be seen as another example of the reciprocal influence of ICTs on human values and human values on ICT environments, as the virtual and morally malleable nature of ICTs may be perceived as simply a means to an end. Hence, moral disengagement is not only dependent on the characteristics of the individual, but also on the context in which an individual is acting – the digital world. As we will see in the next chapter, outputs and inputs, positive and negative feedback while using ICTs affects the morality of young people in the digital world.

CHAPTER THREE

Moral Issues in the Digital World and Moral Reasoning

In chapters three, four and five, I use the findings of my study to show the role of values and behaviours (moral and immoral) with respect to moral reasoning, emotions and behaviours by young people while using ICTs. I have found that some students (a group of 14 to 15 year olds) could reflect critically on moral and immoral issues associated with the use of ICTs, suggesting that this is an important ability. This also helps us understand how the moral domains mediate the use of ICTs and how the moral domains can be fostered.

The CVS model is a teaching and learning tool to stimulate conversations and reflections with students about the role of values in the use of ICTs. Learning can occur when individuals reflect on and critically evaluate the values and practices that mediate their reasoning, emotions and behaviours while using ICTs. The CSV model can be used to foster such reflections. Young people also need to be able to articulate their understanding of how ICTs shape their values and practices, and what ethical standards should shape their practices.

Technologically Mediated Moral Issues

To understand the moral issues associated with the reciprocal immoral influences of humans and ICTs on each other (Technologically Mediated Moral Issues), we will investigate the immoral values that undermine integrity, honesty, trustworthiness, authenticity, accountability (values associated with moral reasoning), empathy and contentiousness (values associated with moral emotion), and self-control, responsibility, altruism, justice and respect (values associated with moral behaviour) – the values that make up the Digital Moral Framework discussed later in the book.

In the list of Technologically Mediated Moral Issues below, immoral values and behaviours identified by students are placed in order of importance with respect to the moral concerns they had while using ICTs. The order of importance is from highest to lowest, based on the 221 instances each moral concern that is expressed by them. The following order of importance emerged:

Technologically Mediated Moral Issues

1. Irresponsibility with respect to how young people portray others – creation of the digital shadow of others).

2. Injustice (cyberbullying, harassment and power over others).

3. Inauthenticity (not being true to who they are).

4. A lack of accountability for one's actions.

5. Dishonesty.

6. A lack of empathy.

7. A lack of self-control.

8. Peer pressure and popularity which affects inappropriate behaviours.

9. Untrustworthiness

10. Irresponsibility (self-made digital shadows).

11. Disrespect.

12. Alack of integrity.

13. Alack conscientiousness.

Technologically Mediated Moral Issues and Moral Reasoning

"You don't think about your values when you post something" – Louise

This section explores the impact of outputs and inputs, negative and positive feedback, and circularity on moral reasoning with respect to students uses of ICTs. The good news is that some young people could understand the impact of both good and detrimental values. Additionally, moral abilities and the teaching and learning methods that can be used to foster moral reasoning are discussed. Table 3.1 at the end of this chapter summarises these processes, abilities and methods. Understanding how these processes foster and undermine moral reasoning is important when seeking to foster morality in the use of ICTs.

The Impact of Moral and Immoral Reasoning on the Digital World

Outputs are the influences that humans have on ICT environments. Students were influenced by the inputs and positive feedback coming from ICT environments, but some resisted these influences. Negative feedback is when inputs coming from ICT environments are assessed and resisted, based on the preferred values of the individual.

The characteristics of learning with respect to negative feedback include the ability to monitor and understand meaningful deviation of one's preferred values, and the ability to resist and correct these deviations. All students in my study could apply some moral values to identify immoral issues associated with the use of ICTs such as, dishonesty, inauthenticity and disingenuous friendships and, in some, instances, resisted these values coming from ICT environments based on their preferred values. Seven out of eight student participants also spoke about their own moral expectation of themselves, suggesting that negative feedback played a beneficial role in their moral reasoning. However, some findings also indicate that inappropriate values and behaviours of young people had a detrimental influence on the moral reasoning of their peers in ICT environments, such as social media.

Honesty and Untrustworthiness

"If you tell someone something about yourself, you don't want them to post it anywhere. Telling other people, it's not lying, it's just passing on information, so they would still be honest but you wouldn't be trusting them" - Betty

Some students appeared to understand that one can be honest, yet lack moral reasoning with respect to protecting the confidentiality of their peers, and therefore not being trustworthy while using ICTs. Also, Louise appeared to question whether some of her peers were being "overly honest" online in order to gain the trust of others, "It'll make you think, is this person actually trustworthy or are they just saying all these things because they're trying to make you feel that way". Tyrone and Tim suggested that being overly honest about others while using ICTs was also a moral concern, as this behaviour hurts others. Tyrone noted, "That's also not very good because honesty hurts and people take that to heart". Other students shared that they wanted to interact with individuals they could trust to not violate their privacy.

Dishonesty

Shouja said that some lie in order to be popular, "Oh, I hang with this person. You probably don't hang with them … you're using their name to get you more friends or more likes. If your value is being the coolest person then you obviously might lie." Tyrone, Tim and Baba commented that some of their peers pretend to be others in order to spread lies and rumours about their peers. Tim told the story of a student that created a fake Facebook account to "pretend to be other people … and tell people lying stuff about themselves." These findings suggest that some students could critically evaluate the immoral influence of dishonesty and untrustworthiness on ICT environments and could critically evaluate lapses in moral reasoning by their peers.

Moral Reasoning - Integrity and Authenticity

"I am a completely different person online depending on who I am talking with" - a student

ICTs are commonly used by high school children to create online profiles. Online identity performances by adolescents often involve a desire to be validated by their peers and meet expectations of peers. Clairie commented that some of her peers, "post something against their values that they think would make them so much better", suggesting that integrity and authenticity are sacrificed for the sake of being approved by one's peers.

ICTs provide the ability for users to manipulate information about themselves more easily and adopt a new persona. Students did not express concern about their peers' creative use of profiles pictures and names; however, they expressed concern about the inauthenticity of how they portrayed themselves online and the disingenuous online friendships of their peers. Louise said, "You could be putting it on… when you're on computers you're a whole, other type."

Several students expressed a desire to have favourable digital images that are a positive reflection of who they are. This is good and important. However, it would appear that the desire to create favourable digital images on the part of adolescents could sometimes lead to the creation of detrimental digital shadows. Betty said, "Well, if someone wants to get a lot of likes on *Facebook*, they have to be not wearing as much clothes as they probably should be, just so they can say, 'Oh, I've got 100 likes on my photo last night.'" One just has to look at social media to understand this. There appeared to be an awareness of circularity by some students that creating inauthentic digital images may lead to an increase in this behaviour because of the approval students received from their peers (positive feedback).

Popularity and Attention Seeking

"The more popular you are, then the more you'll post things online without thinking because it's all peer pressure" – John

Popularity and attention seeking appeared to be major factors for online inauthenticity. Betty said this about popularity. "It's very powerful. There's the saying 'guilty by association', there's 'popular by association.'" "You probably don't hang with them, you're using their name to get you more friends or more likes." Of course, this situation would also be the case in student's offline worlds; however, ICTs may have been a factor that intensifies this behaviour because of the ease with which it can be done using ICTs.

Another concern for young people is that these inauthentic representations are there for many to see and spread. These findings suggest that some students' desire to create digital images that received peer approval appeared to lead to the creation of detrimental digital shadows. Yet, students also showed critical thinking with respect to inauthenticity.

Disingenuous Friendships

"When you go back to school you think you're really good friends with them, but they might ditch you, but that's because they are only good friends while through technology". – Shouja

"You don't really know people just because you know them online". – A student

Some students suggested that some friendships can be disingenuous while using ICTs. It was very common for their peers to be nice online and ignore them at school. Conversely, they could be mean to each other online, yet at school they would act as if nothing had happened. Betty and Shouja suggested that some sacrificed authentic friendships in order to maintain their popularity. Betty also shared a similar experience. "I've had people bullying me over the internet, and then I see them face- to-face, 'Oh, hi, how you going?' It's like, 'You're saying bad things about me over the internet, but then when I see you, you're being all nice to me.'"

The reported lying, pirating content, spreading rumours and violations of privacy, were all examples of deficiencies with respect to honesty, trustworthiness and accountability. However, participants had most to say about a lack of moral reasoning when it came to authenticity. Of the four moral concerns associated in this study with moral reasoning, enactments of inauthenticity in their peers' online profiles and how this could lead to digital shadows for them, and disingenuous friendships by their peers appeared to be the greatest concern for the students.

The Impact of the Digital World on Moral Reasoning

"In year nine we have daily occurrences of students doing silly things and bullying, who are the kind of kids that would never do this in real life. They would say that they have good values but when using ICTs these values are not engaged." – A teacher

This section discusses the influence of ICT environments (inputs and positive feedback) on young peoples' moral reasoning, emotions and behaviours. Positive feedback is when inputs coming from ICT environments cause human values to change and reinforce particular behaviours (good and bad). Some findings suggest that positive feedback had both, a detrimental and a beneficial influence on moral reasoning. Certain characteristics of ICTs such as, diffusion, displacement, anonymity and instrumentality appeared to have a detrimental influence on the values and moral reasoning of some young people. For example, these characteristics appeared to influence moral reasoning with respect to cyberbullying, disrespect, disingenuous friendships, dishonesty, inauthenticity, and a lessened sense of accountability and moral responsibility. Positive feedback from peers in the ICT environment also appeared to encourage inauthentic and inappropriate social media postings, but is some instances peers also encouraged good behaviours. Several student could critically assess the impact of ICTs on moral reasoning.

The Influence of Instrumentality on Moral Reasoning

"It (ICTs) just opens up more ways to do things that are not strictly 100% legal. You don't have the risk and everyone does it anyway. So you just feel like it's not really that much of a bad thing you are doing." - Tyrone

Instrumentality is defined as viewing ICTs as tools that allow us to achieve what we want. Technology seen through the decontextualised and objectified lens of utility (a tool to use) open its use to exploitation. Instrumentality may restrict moral evaluations of the harm done, undermining a sense of moral accountability and responsibility. Some students shared this view. Betty stated, "Yeah, on the internet, people think, 'I can get away with a lot.'" This finding is similar to other research that has found that despite an awareness of the associated ethical or legal problems, most people act dishonestly when they believe that they can get away with it (Blau & Eshet-Alkalai, 2017).

Some of the students' teachers suggested that moral reasoning can be undermined by anonymity and instrumentality, and that there was often some kind of acceptance/justification of this by some students. Robert (a teacher) suggested that students were aware of the risks of their inappropriate online behaviours to themselves, but looked for avenues to avoid detection such as anonymity. Robert provided an example of year nine students using *Snapchat* to bully others. Students would nominate to a friend one of their peers to be attacked using a closed discussion texting application on their mobile phones. The friend was encouraged to share their criticism about the nominated peer. The de-identified screen shot was then sent out to a larger group of students on *Snapchat*. Characteristics of ICTs such as anonymity, lessened socio-emotional cues, displacement/distance from others, and instrumentality appear to influence moral reasoning of students.

Negative feedback and Moral Reasoning

With respect to negative feedback (students following their own values), the recognition by some students of the detrimental influences of certain characteristics of ICTs suggests that this played a role in the moral learning of students. For example, some students appeared to recognise that the outputs from ICT environments, such as diffusion and displacement, instrumentality and anonymity had an influence on moral reasoning and moral behaviour with respect to dishonesty, inauthenticity, a lack of accountability, integrity and moral responsibility. They also appeared to try to safeguard, make moral decisions and take actions based on these values. In addition, some students noted that it was easy to lie on the internet, suggesting that some students understood the influence ICTs had on their values and behaviours. However, the actions of peers in ICT environments (positive feedback) also had a beneficial influence on moral reasoning with respect to honesty.

The Influence of ICTs on Trust

"You'd probably be warier of trusting it, telling people on the internet because if you message someone something that's really private, they have that message and they can ... send it to someone else." - Tyrone

The Influence of Distance and Displacement on Moral Reasoning

Virtual settings alter or even obstruct the process of trust formation. Finding it hard to trust that what is shared online will remain private was another concern expressed by some students. Some students appeared to suggest that distance (behind the screen and keyboard – the shield and the sword) influenced moral reasoning in a detrimental way with respect to how young people portray themselves. Students also appeared to critically reflect on the impact of distance on morality suggesting that this influenced their peers to be 'too honest' about themselves and others while using ICTs.

Clairie provided this advice to her peers, "Don't go out of your way to do something you wouldn't normally say or do. Put it into a real life context and say, 'Would I really do that normally without being behind a computer screen?'"

Louise and Tyrone also suggested that it was sometimes hard to trust their peers because of the influence of ICTs on their moral reasoning. Tyrone said, "If you tell someone something just between you and them, they might go and tell someone else on the internet."

The Influence of ICTs on Authenticity

"People might behave like they normally do in person, but then others may tend to differ from their actual real personality in the real world." - Tim

ICTs dispose individuals to present information in a skewed way to fit their objectives. Thus, ICTs can influence the creation of false self-representations, which may lead young people to present different versions of themselves. Findings suggest that this characteristic of ICTs influenced authenticity in a detrimental way. Shouja shared this view by stating, "That's very strange. Because some people are very kind, more open, some are more angry or upset on that (ICTs)."

Enactments of inauthentic digital images may affect young people's psychological wellbeing, as there may be psychological costs to inconsistency, such as feeling alienated from one's true self, because of a lack of authenticity between one's online and offline selves. These fragmented identities may cause young people frustration because of their inability to reconcile their online and offline selves (Davis et al., 2010). In one study, students (15 to 24 year olds) expressed discomfort about the multiplicity of identities while using ICTs because of interpersonal betrayal and the violation of online social norms (Arıcak, Dündar, & Saldaña, 2015).

Betty also reflected on this phenomenon, stating, "In our generation, a lot they have the term, 'What happens on the internet stays on the internet.' Which I think is just irrational because it's still life." She also added:

> If someone's growing up being two different people on the
> internet and in person, they're going to have split personalities.
> If they're so used to being this way to someone face-to-face,

then being the other way to someone on the internet. Maybe they're going to lose some friends because people have found out who they are really, in both of their lives.

Students appeared to recognised the immoral influence of ICT environments on young peoples' moral reasoning and behaviours. Some students appeared to suggest that digital moral malleability negatively influenced authenticity, integrity, honesty and accountability.

Circularity – The Reciprocal Influence of Humans and the Digital World on Each Other

"What goes around comes around." – Tyrone

"You're more taught things from technology ... You have different values putting things out there, but in most cases, you get the wrong ones back." – Louise

Moral disengagement while using ICTs is dependent on the reciprocal immoral influence of humans on ICTs and the influence of ICTs on moral reasoning - the characteristics of the individual and the context in which an individual is acting. Some students recognised that the creation of inauthentic/fake digital images (outputs), which come with the approval of their peers (inputs and positive feedback), encourages this behaviour. This suggests some level of understanding with respect to the influence of circularity on values, where outputs feed back onto their very cause. Another example of circularity in moral reasoning is remorse. One student noted that a lack of accountability while using ICTs led him and his peers to experience remorse for actions on social media. Some students also appeared to be aware that inappropriate actions while using ICTs could easily feed back onto them. With respect to circularity and the detrimental influence of distance on what his peers posted on social media, Tyrone said, "Well, just like with me, you might be more honest because you just think it might not come back around as much, but it really does." Betty also seemed to understand this issue, stating, "If you're mean on the internet, it could come back to bite you later", while Louise pointed out that if you are driven by bad moods while using ICTs, "That's what you're going to get out of it."

Fostering Moral Reasoning

Some findings suggest that practical wisdom, namely, student awareness and reflections about the influences of negative and positive feedback, and circularity indicate that these processes may have played a role in fostering moral reasoning.

With respect to negative feedback (adhering to one's values), Clairie and John said that inappropriate behaviours by their peers (outputs) highlighted what not to do while using ICTs, maintaining that they could learn from their peers' mistakes.

Because of the potential disconnect between behaviours and the consequences of behaviours while using ICTs, the link between moral reasoning and the consequences of one's behaviours needs to occur. Conscious moral deliberations can lead to new fits being forged between morality and technology, during which values are modified and can settle. Some students described the critical evaluation of their own values and behaviours, while two students and two teachers noted that young people could learn moral lessons from past mistakes while using ICTs, suggesting that conscious deliberation about circularity played a role in moral learning. These types of reflection can lead to the re/construction of knowledge based on life experiences, which can result in new ways of thinking and being. Robert (a teacher) expressed the need for such reflections:

> The moral reasoning in our lives comes from lessons learnt through experience (circularity) and role modelling from adults. This generation does not have many active adult role

models in their technological world and have developed expectations of behaviour that reflect expectations of peers. Being a good cyber citizen is just lip service until there is an experience to shape that understanding.

The findings in this study suggest that discussions with students that stimulate a critical reflection of the values that mediate the use of ICTs with respect to outputs and inputs, negative and positive feedback and circularity may be a means of fostering moral reasoning. Table 3.1 summarises moral reasoning and learning with respect to these processes.

Table 3.1 The CVS Model and Moral Reasoning

Processes	Abilities and learning objectives	Teaching and Learning Methods
Negative Feedback Inputs from ICT environments are assessed and resisted based on the preferred values of the individual	**Outputs**: Reflect critically on immoral issues coming from people into ICT environments Having moral expectations of oneself. **Negative feedback**: Apply moral values to identify moral issues such as dishonesty, inauthenticity and disingenuous friendships.	Discussions and activities that stimulate a critical reflection of the values that mediate the use of ICTs by young people.
Positive feedback Inputs from ICT environments cause human values to change	Identify the detrimental influences of positive feedback coming from ICT environments on moral reasoning such as: diffusion, displacement, anonymity and instrumentality.	Discussions and activities that stimulate critical reflections on the influences of positive feedback on moral reasoning. This can help foster moral learning.

Processes	Abilities and learning objectives	Teaching and Learning Methods
Positive feedback Inputs from ICT environments cause human values to change	How does this shape practices online. Don't look for ways to avoid detection when doing something wrong. Identify influence of ICT environments on moral reasoning with respect to cyberbullying, disrespect, disingenuous friendships, dishonesty, inauthenticity, and a lessened sense of accountability and moral responsibility. Identify how positive feedback from peers may encourage inauthentic and inappropriate postings, but may also encourage moral reasoning and moral behaviour.	Is it easy to lie online? Does distance (behind the keyboard) influence moral reasoning in a detrimental way with respect to how you portray yourself and others online? Does using ICTs restrict moral evaluations of the harm done?

Processes	Abilities and learning objectives	Teaching and Learning Methods
Circularity Actions taken in ICT environments feed back onto its very cause	Being aware that the creation of inauthentic digital images (outputs), which come with the approval of their peers (inputs), encourages this behaviour. Circularity when peer approval of inauthentic public profiles leads to an increase in this behaviour. A lack of accountability while using ICTs leads to remorse for wrong actions. Critically evaluate the inappropriate actions that feed back onto individuals while using ICTs.	Discussions about the influence of circularity on values and behaviours while using ICTs. Discussions and activities that focus on learning from one's mistakes and those of others.

CHAPTER FOUR

Moral Issues in the Digital World and Moral Emotions

"There is distance between you and the other person". - Tim

Moral emotions are self-evaluative (conscience and remorse) and other-oriented emotions (empathy) that support moral reasoning and behaviour. This section discusses the influence of inputs and outputs, negative and positive feedback, and circularity on emotions. Events in the digital world (inputs) have both positive and negative influences on emotions, while young people also act morally in the digital world based on moral values and moral emotions (outputs and negative feedback). Positive feedback from others leads to strengthening the likelihood that good or inappropriate behaviours will continue. I maintain that these processes played a role in fostering moral values and abilities and moral emotions, as well as, undermining them. Table 4.1 summarises the role of these influences with respect to moral abilities, and the teaching and learning methods that can be used to foster moral emotions.

Young people's emotions influence ICT environments for good, yet, also for ill with respect to a lack of empathy and conscientiousness. Additionally, anger, sadness, anxiety and a desire to be popular affected their uses. Conversely,

ICTs also affected their emotions, for good and for ill. Characteristics of ICTs such as anonymity, instrumentality, distance and the dampening of social-emotional affected moral emotions. Students spoke about ICTs as the 'space', 'distance', 'barrier' and 'shield' that distance people from each other, suggesting that ICTs can dampen the empathy felt for others and the remorse felt for inappropriate behaviours.

The Influence of Emotions on the Digital World

"There is always people being hurt over social media and ICT. In some ways it isn't good for people's wellbeing". – Tim

Emotions influence the use of ICTs. For example, moral disengagement with empathy is associated with cyberbullying (Wang et al., 2017). Some students shared that a lack of empathy caused emotional harm to others. Some students said that not being considerate of the feelings of others leads to emotional upsets, anger or sadness in others. Louise shared that when some of her peers post hurtful things, "they don't think about how this could affect other people". These findings suggest that a lack of empathy can mediate the use of ICTs by some young people. Additionally, a lack of empathy was considered the sixth greatest concern by students with respect to the 14 moral concerns studied (see the list of Technologically Mediated Moral Issues in chapter three).

The next section discusses emotional issues such as anxiety, 'bad moods', a desire to be popular and peer pressure, and how these emotions mediated the use of ICTs.

Inappropriate Emotions

"If you're in a bad mood and you go on social media you're out looking for somebody to vent to." – Louise

With respect to the role of burdensome emotions, online forms of anti-social behaviour are associated with depression, anxiety and low levels of self-esteem. Adolescents who report more intense and changeable emotions, and less effective regulation of these emotions have been found to report more problem behaviours while using ICTs (Houck et al., 2014). Several students suggested that emotional states such as anxiety, 'bad moods', a desire to be popular and peer pressure, undermined the use of ICTs by some of their peers.

Attention Seeking and Popularity

"They've got like a popularity scale almost. So, they will do things that they wouldn't normally do." - Clairie

Youth identity exploration and formation are facilitated by self-expression, self-reflection and feedback from others. Feedback from others is a critically important source of validation; however, our reliance on feedback from others may interfere with our own self-reflection. Self-esteem is one of the main predictors of psychological wellbeing. Social self-esteem is largely shaped through interactions with close friends and peers, which often occurs on social media. Positive feedback from friends on social media improves social or global self-esteem, whereas negative feedback from and neglect by friends decreases global and social self-esteem (Valkenburg, Koutamanis, & Vossen, 2017). Another study found that social networking use was higher among people low in self-esteem, high in narcissism and high in loneliness (Baumeister & Liua, 2016).

Some of the concerns noted by students was that attention seeking and peer approval undermined moral reasoning, emotion and behaviour, and how some of their peers portrayed themselves online. Shouja said that the values that many adopt online are based on "whatever makes them seem more popular than others". Betty stated that some of her peers would, "Lie, cheat, make fake things and do bad stuff to get popular… I just think that they want to be accepted into the real world, but then when they're on the internet, they may not be as cool." Some students shared their concern about these ineffective and inappropriate attempts to raise their self-esteem. For example, Betty stated, "Well, if someone wants to get a lot of likes on *Facebook*, they have to be not wearing as much clothes." Findings also suggest that attention seeking and popularity were also reasoned to motivate harassing others. Tim shared that "on *Facebook* there are lots of attention seekers, just hoping to get their little bit of attention and a bit of laugh, but it's not always fun for the other person."

Adopting the Behaviours of Peers and a Lack of Conscientiousness

"Take your friends on the internet, you do adopt their behaviours and what they think 'Oh, yeah. They're doing it; it must be normal.'" - Louise

Several students believed that peer pressure while using ICTs influenced them to go against their own values. Tim claimed that some of his peers "care too much about what other people say", while Betty suggested, "You are sort of going along with the flow, just so that you can have friends and you can be counted as a popular person." Tyrone acknowledged his own shortcomings with respect to a lack of conscientiousness and the remorse he felt when faced with peer pressure to do something that went against his values. "You might still go along with something even though you're not that comfortable with it. You would still feel bad about what you're doing, just not do anything about it".

Anxiety

Research suggests that the more depressed users are, the more they are inclined to do broadcasting activities on social media (Wee, Jang, Lee, & Jang, 2017). Also, people act more irrationally when it comes to self-disclosure of negative life events because of their desire to seek help and release stress, while considering other potential consequences of self-disclosure less rationally (Cho, 2017). Some students shared this concern. Baba noted, "People who have anxiety ... attention seek on social media and they receive sympathy of people."

Negative Feedback and Moral Emotion

Negative feedback occurs when inputs from ICT environments are resisted based on the preferred values of the individual. Negative feedback such as, empathic concern for others appeared to be a factor in the self-reported affective empathy and care some students provided their peers who were cyberbullied or in distress. Cognitive empathy also appeared to play a role in evaluating and managing their own emotions, such as not blaming others. The findings also indicate that some students recognised and understood the harmful emotional experiences of their peers in ICT environments (cognitive empathy).

The Favourable Impact of ICTs on Emotions

Negative events in the digital world triggered empathic concern in some students. For example, the recognition of the harmful emotional experiences of their peers (inputs/events in ICT environments) appeared to be a factor in the empathy/care shown towards their peers.

ICT environments can also have a positive influence on some young peoples' emotions with respect to communication with peers. For young people experiencing difficulties in engaging in social relationships, online anonymity may lower the barriers to meeting new friends (Heirman & Walrave, 2008) and increase greater freedom of expression (Heesen, 2012). The anonymity provided by ICTs enabled a greater freedom of expression for some young people who were less confident in communicating within the real world. Baba noted that "this one girl was sarcastic, witty and maybe a bit obnoxious online, but at school she was really shy. Some students can express themselves more easily online." Louise, Betty, Tim and Shouja commented that ICTs allowed some of their peers to communicate more easily. Louise stated that "when somebody is talking on social media or just texting, they will be open to you and then you can be open back to them". Betty argued that some of her peers were more confident to share while being anonymous. The anonymity allowed them to overcome their shyness, share their feelings more openly and get support from others. Betty stated, "If they post it anonymously, there's people to give them support without knowing who they are". Betty also claimed:

> You can communicate on the technology easier than you can face-to- face, like you may mumble your words when you're talking face-to-face but on the internet you can backspace, you can autocorrect. Some people can be more confident on the internet. They can say things that they wouldn't generally say to someone's face.

The Immoral Influence of the Digital World on Moral Emotions

"In real life you say something and you can see the look on people's faces, whether they approve or disapprove of what you're saying, so you can accommodate what you're talking about." - Louise

This section discusses findings in relation to the immoral impact of ICT environments on cognitive empathy and conscience. First, characteristics of ICTs (inputs), such as diffusion and displacement of responsibility create an emotional gap while using ICTs, which in turn, appears to impact the level of empathy and concern felt for others, and anti-social behaviours. One study found that distance from others while using ICTs minimises the consequences of actions on others, which influenced moral disengagement. Additionally, the emotional gap that is created lessened socio-emotional cues, which reduces the emotional consequences (remorse) of aggressive acts. Empathy relies, in part, on sensory emotional cues. Removing nonverbal cues, such as tone of voice, eliminates one of the conditions for the elicitation of empathy while using ICTs (Runions & Bak, 2015).

Second, several students argued that peer pressure (positive feedback) undermined the moral domains of some of their peers. Positive feedback in social relations can lead to strengthening particular behaviours. One study found that when young people become overly dependent on the validation of their peers, it undermined how they portrayed themselves online (Davis et al., 2010). Some students also noted the dampening of emotional cues while using ICTs and its influence on the empathy felt for others. Other findings suggest that remorse for hurting others or pirating music were also dampened while using ICTs.

Lessened Empathy

Students suggested that the dampening of sensory emotional cues affected the level of empathy and concern felt for others and increased the anti-social behaviours of some of their peers. However, it is not clear whether these recognitions influenced the empathy they felt or showed to others. Betty said that empathy was not often present because it was hard to determine who was in need while using ICTs and that it was easier to exclude people online. "I don't know what it's doing to them, so I don't care. No one will know that you're hurt."

She also said:

> It doesn't happen a lot [empathy] because everyone just looks at them and be like, 'They're fine, they're all right'. We don't see the people's reaction to it. Seeing people's reaction would flick a switch maybe to be like, if that's how they're reacting I probably shouldn't say [rude] things like that.

Cyberbullying

"Some people may find it easier to put someone down or lie when you're not doing it to the face, because they can't see your body language or facial expressions. They don't know from their other side if it's probably developing into anger or sadness."

Shouja

The invisibility of the victim might be a specific feature of cyberbullying that is important to consider, as there is an increased probability that the bully does not directly see the emotional impact of his/her actions on the victim, at least not in the immediate exchange (Perren & Gutzwiller-Helfenfinger, 2012). Additionally, a lack of visual ques may make deception easier (Davis et al., 2010).

Betty said that it was very common for her peers to say things on social media that they would not necessarily say, face to face. On three different occasions, Louise made similar statements:

> I think when you're on social media and technology you don't really think about it as much as you would if you're talking to someone in person". You're like, I don't really care, I can say something meaner. You don't think about whether it would have an effect. Would this hurt another person? Emotionally would this upset this person that I'm putting this photo up?

Remorse

"On the internet, people think, I can get away with a lot." Betty

Several studies have indicated that bullying is associated with lower levels of remorse (Perren & Gutzwiller-Helfenfinger, 2012). Distance also appeared to affect the level of remorse felt by students. Tyrone noted that, "someone's not really there you're not going to feel bad about hurting someone if you don't see them hurt."

Circularity, Empathy and Conscience

Circularity is when an effect feeds back onto its very cause. Some students spoke about the remorse they and their peers felt about inappropriate actions while using social media, suggesting that circularity played a favourable role in the evaluation of students' emotions and behaviours towards others. The role of emotions in circularity also appeared to undermine moral reasoning and moral behaviour. For example, Clairie claimed, "If you are emotional, you may make rash decisions." Some students also indicated that their peers would post pictures of themselves that were revealing (outputs), to get more likes on *Facebook*, suggesting that peer approval (inputs and positive feedback) of these postings played a role in reinforcing this behaviour. Some students suggested that it was easier to lie and hurt others because of the distance between individuals while using ICTs, suggesting that circularity can undermine the moral domains. The characteristics of ICTs (inputs) that make it easier to lie and hurt others influenced the values of some young people, which led to an increase in these immoral values being enacted in ICT environments (outputs).

Fostering Empathy and Conscience

This section discusses the influence of outputs and inputs, negative and positive feedback, and circularity on fostering empathy and conscience. Emotional experiences in real-life situations can be used as a basis for children's moral learning. The use of ICTs is a reoccurring, real-life setting for young people to experience, reflect on and practice empathy and conscience. Fostering these is influenced in part by: 1) reasoning with regard to empathy and remorse; 2) learning to consider the perspective of others;

3) self-awareness and self-evaluation of one's behaviours; and 4) taking an active interest in the concerns of others.

Empathy and conscience are self-evaluative emotions. For example, the emotional discomfort (remorse) following a behaviour that is in opposition to one's own moral values fosters reasoning and self-evaluation. Some findings suggest that the processes of outputs and inputs, negative and positive feedback and circularity while using ICTs had an influence on eliciting/fostering self-evaluative emotions such as empathy and remorse. With respect to negative feedback, some students appeared to have the ability to assess inputs coming from ICT environments based on empathy and remorse, and reported taking some actions (outputs) based on these values. Some students also reported taking an active interest in the suffering of their peers. These processes may have played a role in fostering empathy and remorse. Taking the perspectives of others and understanding that moral transgressions have a negative influence on others are factors that foster empathy and remorse. Students' perception of the experiences of their peers appeared to influence some student's ability to take their peers perspective, understand what they were experiencing and feeling, and understand that moral transgressions had negative consequences on their peers. Circularity also played a role in fostering self-assessment of one's action towards others with respect to empathy and remorse.

Table 4.1 summarises the role of outputs and inputs, positive and negative feedback, and circularity with respect to moral abilities and the teaching and learning methods that can be used to foster moral emotions.

Table 4.1 - The CVS Model and Moral Emotions

Processes	Abilities and Learning Objectives	Teaching and Learning Methods
Negative Feedback Inputs from ICT environments are assessed and resisted based on the values of empathy and remorse.	Cognitive empathy relies on (a) taking another person's perspective, (b) understanding what others are experiencing and feeling, and (c) recognising the harmful emotional experiences of others in ICT environments. Caring for others who are bullied or in distress. Identifying and describing the factors that influence your emotional responses.	Discussions and activities with regard to inputs coming from ICT environments based on the values of empathy and remorse. Fostering moral emotions is influenced in part by: 1) reasoning with regard to empathy and remorse 2) learning to consider the perspective of others 3) self-awareness and self-assessment of one's behaviours 4) taking an active interest in the concerns of others.

Processes	Abilities and Learning Objectives	Teaching and Learning Methods
Positive Feedback Inputs from ICT environments cause human values to change	Students' perception of the experiences of their peers appeared to influence some student's ability to take their peers perspective, understand what they were experiencing and feeling, and understand that moral transgressions had negative consequences on them. Recognising that peer pressure can undermine the moral domains, but also support them. Being aware of the dampening of emotional cues and its influence on empathy and remorse while using ICTs.	Discussions and activities with regard to inputs coming from ICT environments based on the values of empathy and remorse in order to take another person's perspective and understand what others are experiencing. Discussions and activities about the dampening of emotional cues while using ICTs and its influence on empathy and remorse.

Processes	Abilities and Learning Objectives	Teaching and Learning Methods
Circularity Actions taken in ICT environments feed back onto its very cause	Understanding the role of circularity in how inappropriate behaviours feedback on to oneself based on the values of empathy and remorse. Understanding that peer approval can play a role in reinforcing both inappropriate and appropriate behaviours. Understanding how the characteristics of ICTs can influence empathy and lead to inappropriate behaviours towards others.	Discussing the role of circularity with respect to a self-assessment of one's action towards others with respect to empathy and remorse.

CHAPTER FIVE

Moral Issues in the Digital World and Moral Behaviours

In this chapter we look at the reciprocal influence of human values on ICT environments and the influence of ICT environments on human values with respect to moral behaviours. Moral behaviour is analysed based on two dimensions: moral self-management, which relies on self-control and responsibility, and moral behaviour towards others, based on the values of altruism, justice and respect. Table 5.1 summarises the role of outputs and inputs, positive and negative feedback and circularity with respect to moral abilities, and the teaching and learning methods that can be used to foster the moral behaviour.

Inappropriate values and behaviours (outputs) by young people, such as a lack of self-control, irresponsibility and injustice affected others in ICT environments in a detrimental way. Conversely, moral actions based on self-control, responsibility and justice shows the beneficial role negative feedback (preferred values) played in the moral use of ICTs by some students. Inputs and positive feedback from ICT environments can also have a detrimental influence on moral behaviour. Students suggested that techniques (inputs) (persistence, replicability, scalability and anonymity) influenced responsibility, justice and respect. Positive feedback - inputs from

ICT environments also have a beneficial moral impact on moral learning and behaviour.

Circularity had a detrimental influence on moral behaviour. The desire to create positive digital images can lead to deceptive and inappropriate representations that can lead to undermining self-reflection. Also, self-made digital shadows appeared to undermine personal autonomy and public identities of some young people.

The Influence of Immoral Behaviours on the Digital World

A lack of moral self-management with respect to self-control and responsibility was suggested by some students to adversely affect moral behaviour.

Self-Made Digital Shadows

"When they put something on Facebook, they just write something big about themselves, but you don't realise that you might not want everybody to know about that... and how much of an effect that this is going to have on them." - Louise

Self-definition is considered important for adolescents, as it is through this process that they arrive at their sense of identity (Buckingham, 2008). Students expressed their concerns about irresponsible moral reasoning and behaviours with respect to portraying oneself in a detrimental way using ICTs (self-made digital shadows). Young peoples' digital images were undermined by their own behaviours. This situation could explain, in part, why irresponsibility was the highest ranked moral concern for student participants.

Some students appeared to understand the impact of adopting the wrong values and reasoning (popularity with peers and irresponsibility) on the creation of self-made digital shadows. Louise said, "I saw a person, he was very opinionated in what he said, but he immediately deleted the post but … He got a lot of people disliking him." Tyrone also shared this about self-made digital shadows: "Looking back to your *Facebook* posts and realising that you were that much of an idiot. All the things that you said mean to people … a lot of people can relate to that." Betty said she knew of a girl who lost her reputation by posting an inappropriate picture of herself. "She tried to get it back but she couldn't and then all these boys got it."

A Lack of Self-Control

"There's just not enough people that have self-control. Maybe they just see someone they don't like and just say it on a social media site" - Tim

Some psychologists maintain that self-control involves the ability to suppress inappropriate emotions and actions in favour of appropriate ones. Self-control therefore requires goal-directed behaviour in the face of important, competing inputs and actions (Casey, 2015; Goleman, 2004). Some students considered self-control important for managing what young people post on social media and do in the digital world. However, they also expressed the view that self-control is not a value and behaviour adopted by most of their peers.

While discussing self-control with Clairie (now in year 12), she said that self-control was important because some of her peers used social media to personally attack others when arguments break out. Some students also suggested that a lack of self-control on social media could lead to a breakdown in friendships. Tim said that in order to safeguard relationships, young people needed to resist "the urge to say something nasty." During a classroom discussion, two students commented on self-control, saying that "it's hard to maintain self-control in some situations" and that "this is important, since once it's on the internet, it can't be taken off." Injustices perpetrated through malicious digital shadows created by others and cyberbullying were also of great concern. Students considered self-control important for managing anti-social behaviours.

Injustice and Digital Shadows

"To be honest I hate you, go away, stop liking." – A student

Students spoke about how some of their peers deliberately misused ICTs to disrespect and humiliate others, air disputes, act out revenges and destroy the reputation of others through lies, derogative postings and rumours. Baba also shared that "a lot of revenge" is going on in social media, while John said that some take the anger they experience in their lives and act it out online in the form of cyberbullying. Louise and Tim said that some of their peers made up rumours about others and posted embarrassing photos on social media that humiliate their peers. Tim noted that this led to some of his peers being depressed and closing social media accounts - "It just gave that person a really bad reputation." Tyrone and Clairie suggested possible mindsets that lead to this online behaviour; their peers lacked a sense of justice and were cowards hiding behind the keyboard.

The Influence of Moral Behaviours on the ICT Environments

Some students appeared to be able to determine some moral actions based on self-control and responsibility. A self-awareness of a lack of self-control and responsibility indicates the beneficial role negative feedback (the preferred values of self-control and responsibility) played in the moral use of ICTs for some students, as students were able to reflect on the importance of these values for their behaviours. There were also some self-reported instances of students behaving altruistically and standing up to cyberbullies, suggesting that negative feedback and outputs (moral agency) played a role in how some students responded to events (inputs) coming from ICT environments.

Negative feedback also appeared to influence moral reasoning with respect to the welfare and rights of others, which had a beneficial influence on moral behaviour.

The Immoral Influence of the Digital World on Moral Behaviour

"ICTs allow you to bend your morals." – John

This section discusses the findings about the immoral influence of ICT environments on moral behaviour. Outputs and positive feedback had a detrimental influence on moral behaviours, in two ways.

First, students suggested that digital moral malleability – the virtual and logically malleable characteristics of ICTs that allow us to be "flexible with our morals" influenced responsibility, justice and respect, and how their peers played out power relations online. Characteristics such as anonymity, distance and instrumentality appeared to have a detrimental influence on the values, a sense of moral responsibility and moral behaviours of young people. Some students spoke of ICTs being like "a sword and a shield" which provide the ability to attack others anonymously.

Second, detrimental digital shadows and violations of privacy undermined the wellbeing, personal autonomy, self-definition and formation of adolescents' public identities and self-esteem. This was made worst by the characteristics such as persistence, replicability (spread-ability), search-ability, and scalability (wide visibility and availability) of inappropriate content posted online. This is having a detrimental impact on young people (Boyd, 2014; Flores & James, 2013). They also shared their concern about their loss of control of their information.

Commercial Interests

Commercial deployment of ICTs are shaped by the "interests" and biases of the people who produce and control them, and these, in turn, affect social systems. Some student participants expressed concern that these embedded techniques/code/algorithms could undermine their personal autonomy, privacy and public identities. For example, Betty and Tim shared their concern about the loss of control of their own personal content (persistence, replicability and scalability) such as their inability to remove content.

Persistence, Replicability and Scalability

"What you put out there, it's always going to be there. You're never going to be able to get it back." – Louise

With respect to persistence, replicability and scalability of digital shadows, the findings suggest that some students were concerned about this. Several students expressed the view that "once you press send, you can't get it back," "if you say it on *Facebook*, it's always there to remind that person" and "there's always a record on the IT." Six student interviewees noted the regret they and their peers felt about inappropriate posts on social media. Tyrone shared, "Well, just like with me you might be more honest because you just think it might not come back around as much, but it really does. It's actually worse, because you have a physical state of what you said. ... Even when you delete something, it's not deleted."

The Persistence and Visibility of Cyberbullying

"I think it hurts more (when bullied online) because you can look at it and you subconsciously just read it over and over again and it makes you feel worse."

Louise

"These conversations are happening online for the whole world to see." – Spencer (a parent)

Some research indicates that on social media, interpersonal positive or negative feedback on the self is often more public than in comparable face-to-face settings, which may make adolescents more susceptible to such feedback than comparable feedback in face-to-face settings. Positive feedback from friends improves social or global self-esteem, whereas negative feedback from and neglect by friends decreases global and social self-esteem (Valkenburg et al., 2017). Bullying online makes these dynamics more visible and more persistent.

The persistence and visibility of cyberbullying leave traces of cruel teen interactions. Others can see what is happening and this visibility enables individuals to amplify these attacks. Such heightened visibility can significantly increase the emotional duress of a bullying incident (Boyd, 2014). Some students expressed their concern about the persistence and visibility of cyberbullying. Betty said:

> If you're mean on the internet, it could come back to bite you later, because that comment will always be there. It's always there to remind that person. Anyone can take it and twist it around. …we've seen the effects of what can happen if you do put something out there that you probably shouldn't.

Distance – The Shield

"When they use that computer and stuff, that's kind of a shield, they can say what they really think to people". Tyrone

Another example of the influence of digital moral malleability on moral behaviour is the distancing of one's actions from their effects on others, which can destabilise relationships with others. The virtual nature of the interactions while using ICTs causes individuals to perceive their actions as less 'real', hence distancing individuals from their actions (Floridi, 1999; Nissenbaum, 1994; Runions & Bak, 2015; Wong, 1995).

Some students provided some examples of this phenomenon. They said that for some of their peers, it was easier to put others down online and share their opinions. They also said that the level of respect declines when their peers use ICTs, indicating the influence of ICTs on values and behaviours. Louise shared:

> If you're talking to someone you'd be respectful to them. No matter if you like them or not you're respectful, but when you're on social media or technology you're sort of not. You're talking to a computer screen, not as much a person, so you forget what your values are and how you treat people. It's easy just to vent and just get all your thoughts out there, but you don't think of the consequences.

Anonymity and Invisibility

"You have that opportunity to be able to do things that aren't okay or aren't seen as the right thing to do, but you have that anonymity just to do it and know that you can get away with it." - Tyrone

Another example of the influence of digital moral malleability on moral behaviour is the anonymity provided by ICTs, which has also been referred to as invisibility (Perren & Gutzwiller-Helfenfinger, 2012). Thanks to the anonymity, real identities and actions are separated from the real world. People can create anonymous account on Facebook, Instagram, Snapchat, and other platforms by using a 'Burner Email Account'.

Some researchers have speculated that anonymity may have a disinhibition effect (Flores & James, 2013), that may detrimentally influence on a personal commitment to moral values (Bats, Valkenburg, & Verbeek, 2013; Davis et al., 2010; Yoon, 2011). It is known to increase the likelihood that people will transgress rules and laws and increases aggression.

Students were concerned about anonymity being used by some of their peers to create digital shadows for others and to cyberbully. They shared that some of their peers created anonymous social media accounts to destroy the reputation of others. Additionally, anonymity appeared to detrimentally influence moral engagement. Tyrone and Betty suggested that anonymity in social media influenced their peers' sense of caring and caused some to treat others unjustly. Tyrone noted, "Some people will go to a lot of trouble to hide who they are online so they can say what they want and do what they want." Tim said, that a student in his cohort created an anonymous *Facebook* account called "Honest Bob". "Every week they would post lists basically of who's the hottest or not". Tyrone also spoke about this incident. "Some people were like who's the most hated and who's the ugliest." Betty maintained:

> You can't predict what people are going to do on the internet because this person maybe the nicest person you ever meet and they could have an anonymous account online where they trash people. They'll be mean to people and you could never know because they have no links to reality.

Loss of Control and Privacy

"If you put a photo out there, even if you delete it, people can save it, people can share it and you have no control over what they do with it." - Betty

The broad exposure of information is making privacy more salient for young people. They may be feeling that their identity, reputation and sense of safety are increasingly beyond their control. Because of this, young people may be more aware of the need to carefully manage what they disclose while using ICTs. Six students shared concerns about the immoral influence of persistence, replicability, scalability and loss of control of their information on their privacy.

Louise said, "Anyone can get to it, anyone can see exactly what you're doing." Tyrone also expressed his concern about the impact of a lack of privacy on online relationships. "If you tell someone something just between you and them they might go and tell someone else on the internet."

Self-Control

"If you are on technology you can go out of your limits and think that was too far but you can't control it because of someone else doing it to you as well." – Betty

Most students indicated that ICTs play a role in undermining self-control because of the lack of boundaries. Louise held this view:

> It's easy just to vent and just get all your thoughts out there.
> When you're face-to- face, you have limits, in the real world
> you have limits and you think about things more. When you
> are on a computer, you just say it and hope it works out.

Tyrone referred to his peers not adopting the value of self-control, saying that, "they probably don't feel a need to because there's nobody there to tell them off and tell them they are doing the wrong thing, so why do you need to control yourself if there's not a reason to." Tyrone's reason supports the view that moral self-regulation requires triggers to be activated, which online settings provide little of (Runions & Bak, 2015). This view was also shared in the classroom, with one student stating, "I don't have self-control online mainly because there aren't many boundaries."

The Moral Influence of ICT Environments on Students

ICT environments also had a beneficial influence on moral behaviour. For example, there were some self-reported instances of students responding to cyberbullying by supporting the victim. Hence, events in ICT environments may have played a role in fostering justice and reducing the impact of cyberbullying. Online peer pressure may have played a role in fostering values. Promoting the common good using ICTs was also suggested as a means of fostering altruism.

Circularity and Moral Behaviour

Circularity has a detrimental influence on moral behaviour. A study of young peoples' uses of ICTs suggests that the creation of digital images can lead to deceptive and inappropriate representations that can lead to undermining self-reflection (Davis et al., 2010). Some students suggested that a lack of responsibility and self-control of some of their peers, accompanied by a desire to be popular resulted in self-made digital shadows, which appeared to undermine personal autonomy and public identities of some of their peers. Baba shared an example of a new girl who joined one of her classes at school. Baba and her friend, immediately looked up the new girl's *Instagram* account to determine the type of person she was; "That happens a lot. You get an impression of who they are. For example, if they post a racy picture, or they have pictures with a lot of friends, they appear sociable."

Circularity and Standing Up to Cyberbullies

"If there's bullying, they all want to be in the conversation... but while they're helping the person they were really terrible to the other person." - Baba

Another phenomenon reported by the students was that their peers would stand up to bullies, only to then go on and bully others themselves. Tim commented on this, stating, "They put their nose in and try to help ... but they can end up harassing others". Betty reflected on parents' and peers' encouragement of young people to stand up for themselves online, but questioned whether this advice can lead to cyberbullying. Her parents told her to "stick up for yourself, don't let anyone put you down, so you could be thinking, "'That means I can put them down?'" This situation is another example of the reciprocal immoral influence of ICT environments on values and the influence of student values on ICT environments.

A teacher provided an example of the importance of self-control with respect to circularity, suggesting that students who lacked self-control perpetuated argument and anger, while those who had self-control, short-circuited arguments and anger. Peer approval also appeared to play a role in reinforcing inappropriate and appropriate behaviours.

Fostering Moral Behaviour

The moral reasoning and agency displayed by some students suggest an awareness on their part of the importance of self-control, responsibility, altruism, justice and respect. Additionally, negative feedback (values held by students) appeared to play a role in how some students responded to inputs coming from ICT environments. For instance, moral reasoning about the welfare and rights of others appeared to encourage this moral behaviour. Values education research has found that moral and social knowledge emerges from the child's interactions in the social world. Some students' awareness of their values (negative feedback) and their perceptions of their peers' actions and experiences in ICT environments (inputs) may have played a role in fostering moral reasoning and moral behaviour, which suggests that a critical evaluation of the values and behaviours that mediate the use of ICTs may be a factor in fostering moral behaviour.

An awareness on the part of some students, that persistence, replicability, scalability, distancing and anonymity had an impact on behaviours and the social wellbeing of young people, suggests that discussing these with students may be a means of fostering moral behaviour.

Learning from Circularity

A study of the use of ICTs by young people found that positive feedback from peers can also play a role in fostering moral behaviours (Davis et al., 2010). The findings on justice and respect indicate that online peer pressure (positive feedback) appeared to be at work to foster these values in some students.

A study of morality in the use of ICTs by secondary school students, found that while using ICTs, the consequences of actions (circularity) appeared to provoke a shift in moral reasoning with regard to considering others (Bats et al., 2013). This study points to the role of circularity in moral learning. In my study, some students appeared to understand the consequences of their actions, suggesting a shift in moral reasoning. Also, students' awareness and self-assessment of the impact of a lack of responsibility and self-control suggest that some students understood the detrimental influence of circularity on moral behaviour, indicating that some moral learning occurred through the process of circularity.

Table 5.1 summarises the role of outputs and inputs, positive and negative feedback and circularity with respect to moral abilities, and the teaching and learning methods that can be used to foster the moral behaviour.

Table 5.1 The CVS Model and Moral Behaviour

Processes	Abilities and Learning Objectives	Teaching and Learning Methods
Outputs The influence of people on ICT environments	**Moral self-management** Being aware of the influence of a lack of self-control and responsibility on how we portray ourselves. Being aware of Self-Made Digital Shadows Applying self-control and responsibility to manage and determine moral behaviours. Resist the urge to say or do something wrong. **Moral behaviour towards others** Being aware of injustices perpetrated through digital shadows created by others and cyberbullying Having moral agency by behaving altruistically and standing up to cyberbullies.	Discussions and activities that promote an awareness of one's values and experiences of peers. Discussions and activities that focus on learning from a critical evaluation of the values and behaviours that mediate the use of ICTs.
Negative Feedback Inputs from ICT environments are assessed and resisted based on preferred values	**Moral self-management** Determine moral actions based on self-control and responsibility (negative feedback). A self-awareness of a lack of self-control and responsibility indicates the beneficial role negative feedback (preferred values) played in the moral use of ICTs **Moral behaviour towards others** Behaving altruistically and standing up to cyberbullies, suggesting that negative feedback (moral agency) played a role in how some students responded to inputs coming from ICT environments.	

Processes	Abilities and Learning Objectives	Teaching and Learning Methods
Inputs The influence of ICTs on moral behaviours	Being aware of the influence of persistence, replicability, scalability, distancing, diffusion and displacement, anonymity and instrumentality on moral behaviour and the wellbeing of others. The heightened visibility of bullying and digital shadows can significantly increase the emotional hurt. Being aware that bullying online is more visible and persistent Being aware that digital shadows are more visible and persistent Being aware of what we disclose while using ICTs Being aware of the beneficial effects of positive feedback, such as standing up to bullies Being aware of the detrimental effects of positive feedback. Such as while using ICTs, it is easier to put others down online, how anonymity and Invisibility affects your behaviour. Exerting positive peer pressure with regard to justice and respect. Using ICTs to promote altruism.	Discussions and activities about the influence of persistence, replicability, scalability, distancing and anonymity on the social wellbeing of young people.
Positive Feedback Inputs from ICT environments cause human values to change		Discussions and activities about the role of positive peer pressure in moral behaviour.

Processes	Abilities and Learning Objectives	Teaching and Learning Methods
Circularity Actions taken in ICT environments feed back onto its very cause	Being aware that inappropriate representations can lead to undermining self-reflection Being aware that a desire to be popular can result in self-made digital shadows. Being aware that argument, anger and bullying will continue if people perpetuate them. Being aware of the detrimental influence of circularity with respect to a lack of self-control, responsibility, justice and respect. For example, a lack of self-control and responsibility can feedback onto its very cause in the form of self-made digital shadows.	Discussions and activities that focus on assessing the consequences of one's actions on others. Consequences of actions provoke a shift from self-centred thinking, to considering the welfare of others. Discussions and activities that focus on identifying circularity in moral behaviours.

CHAPTER SIX

Integrity – Values and Moral Reasoning in the Digital World

T his chapter presents the values and abilities that underpin moral reasoning, and how these can be fostered as outlined in the Digital Moral Framework (DMF). The DMF uses the labels of *integrity, heart and character* to explain the values and abilities associated with the moral reasoning, moral emotions and moral behaviours.

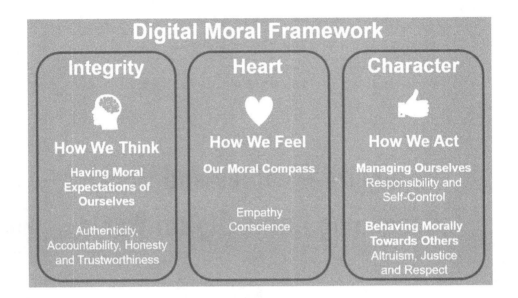

Integrity

In the DMF, *integrity* represents moral reasoning. Integrity is having moral expectation of oneself and living up to one's moral values while using ICTs, based on the values of authenticity, accountability, honesty and trustworthiness.

Heart

In the DMF, *heart* represents moral emotion. Heart is being empathetic towards others and following one's conscience with respect to one's actions while using ICTs.

Character

In the DMF, *character* represents moral behaviour. Character while using ICTs is managing ourselves based on the values of self-control and responsibility, and behaving morally towards others is based on the values of altruism, justice and respect.

With respect to self-management, findings indicate that students ranked a lack of responsibility towards others first and self-control forth out of 14 moral issues. With respect to behaving morally towards others, altruism and justice are ranked second and third by students (see Table 6.1 below).

Student Order of Importance of Values		
Moral Behaviour	1	Responsibility - 16.33%
Moral Behaviour	2	Altruism - 12.24%
Moral Behaviour	3	Justice - 11.66%
Moral Behaviour	4	Self-control - 10.50%
Moral Reasoning	5	Authenticity - 8.75%
Moral Reasoning	6	Accountability - 8.75%
Moral Behaviour	7	Respect - 7.00%
Moral Emotion	8	Empathy - 7.00%
Moral Reasoning	9	Honesty - 6.41%
Moral Reasoning	10	Integrity - 4.66%
Moral Reasoning	11	Trustworthiness - 4.08%
Moral Emotion	12	Conscientiousness - 2.33%

Table 6.1 represents the ranking of importance the students placed on each of the 12 values studied. These values were cited by students in interviews and classroom activities, 343 times.

Integrity and Moral Reasoning in the Digital World

This section discusses the importance of authenticity, accountability, honesty and trustworthiness in relation to moral reasoning, followed by a discussion of some abilities associated with these values. This section also discusses how these values and moral reasoning abilities can be fostered.

Integrity

"If we're trying to tell someone to have good values, we've got to make sure we've got good values… If you've got values, stick to them." – Betty

Seven out of eight student interviewees spoke about their own sense of integrity while using ICTs. Tyrone said, "Do the right thing. Just because everyone else is not, you still have a choice." Clairie and Louise, also indicated their desire to hold themselves accountable to their own values and recommended that their peers do the same. Some students appeared to demonstrate a level of moral reasoning with regard to their own sense of integrity while using ICTs in that they displayed moral expectations of themselves. During the 2017 teacher focus group, the teachers seemed particularly concerned about students' low order of importance of honesty (9th), integrity (10th) and trustworthiness (11th) (see Table 6.1). They expressed concern that there was a disconnect between the stated values of students and their actual behaviours. These findings are similar to studies that suggests that online interactions may be susceptible to a disconnect between moral reasoning and behaviours (Davis et al., 2010; Flores & James, 2013). However, during a student focus group discussion, Clairie and Baba (now in year 12) disagreed with the teachers. Baba noted, "If you had good values, you would practise them". The maturity of year 12 students and good character of these students may have been a factor, and while their views on this disconnect may be admirable, adults generally recognise that the disconnect between values held, and actual behaviours is a common human experience. Woody (a teacher) argued that the problem might be that the current generation of users are growing up with ICTs before they can engage with moral reasoning about values.

Authenticity and ICTs

"I am the same on the internet as I am in real life" "I don't try to look better." – A student

One definition of authenticity while using ICTs is being who we truly are and being consistent in one's self-presentations. Students often noted that authenticity was important for themselves and their peers, indicating the importance of being consistent in how they portrayed themselves online. Some students expressed the view that they wanted to be 'true to themselves' and how they portrayed themselves on social media.

Inauthenticity and a lack of accountability were ranked in third and fourth positions with respect to the 14 moral concerns identified by student (see the list of Technologically Mediated Moral Issues in chapter three). However, in 2017, some of these students, now in year 12, noted that having two personalities, one in the real world and one online, was not as big a concern for them. They argued that being selective in how they portrayed themselves online was not inauthentic, but a mature response to protecting their privacy.

Accountability and ICTs

"A lot of people will go back to what they've said on Facebook … and say 'Why was I was such an idiot?'" Tyrone

Overall, accountability was ranked sixth by students. Betty summed up the need for accountability by saying that "in our generation we have a saying. 'What happens on the internet stays on the internet.'" In this comment, Betty suggests that a potential lack of accountability while using ICTs was a normal occurrence in her cohort.

Some students also appeared to link a lack of accountability to inappropriate behaviours while using social media. Accountability can be considered one of the key values that needs to mediate moral reasoning. For parents and teachers, accountability was ranked low, possibly because they did not understand the implications of this value from the student's point of view. The findings show that responsibility and accountability are considered very important by students because of their lived experiences with respect to the lack of responsibility and accountability on the part of their peers resulting in cyberbullying and digital shadows. There is a link between integrity, authenticity and accountability because students had moral expectations of themselves.

Honesty, Trustworthiness and ICTs

"Honesty is very important because people can't see if you're being honest (behind the screen). They just have to trust that you're being honest." - Betty

Some students considered honesty to be an important value. However, the overall order of importance for honesty for them was not high (9th), yet honesty was important in the use of ICTs for particular reasons, as we can see from Betty's comment above. Honesty was also reasoned by some students to act as a protective measure while using ICTs. For example, Louise suggested that honesty alleviates problems while using ICTs, noting, "You're not going to get yourself into as many little problems."

It appeared that students demonstrated some sophistication in the measured use of honesty while using ICTs. In some situations, honesty was not always considered the "best policy". Betty, for example, maintained that not disclosing private information while using ICTs is appropriate in some situations in order to protect oneself and others: "If someone tells you something that they don't want you to share, you cannot share that but still be honest." Considering that some students were aware that honesty was not always the best policy while using ICTs, this may explain, in part, why honesty was not considered by the students to be as important as other values.

Moral Reasoning Abilities in the Digital World

"Take your friends on the internet you do adopt their behaviours and what they think ... Sometimes you'll be a lot more critical and think whether you want to or not."

– Louise

This section discusses the abilities and learning objectives associated with integrity, authenticity and accountability, and to moral reasoning. Some students had some abilities with respect to authenticity and accountability, namely they could: 1) identify moral issues and make moral judgements based on these values; 2) have moral expectations of themselves, which rely on self-awareness and self-evaluation of one's own values and behaviours; 3) justify moral judgements and 4) determine moral actions based on these values. These abilities also apply to moral emotion and moral behaviour.

Identifying Moral Issues, Making Moral Judgements and Having Moral Expectations

If we're trying to tell someone to have good values, we've got to make sure we've got good values.... If you've got values, stick to them." - Betty

Betty's comments suggests a sense of authenticity and accountability, and moral expectations of herself. Making moral judgements with respect to ICTs requires applying moral values to identify moral issues associated with ICTs. Some students could apply moral values (authenticity and accountability) to identify moral issues and made moral judgements associated with the use of ICTs, and appeared to have some moral expectations of themselves while using ICTs. The findings on integrity, honesty, trustworthiness, authenticity and accountability suggest that many of the students applied some moral values to make moral choices and in some instances could justify their choices. For example, in order to protect their peers, students did not disclose private information and were aware of the need to be authentic in the digital world. This also suggests that some students had some self-awareness and self-evaluation of their own values and behaviours.

As indicated in the section on the influence of moral reasoning on ICT environments, some students could critically evaluate a lack of integrity, authenticity, honesty and accountability with respect to moral reasoning while using ICTs. They could also evaluate the inauthentic and detrimental digital shadows, and disingenuous friendships created online and determine a moral action for themselves. As suggested in Louise's comment, "Like, when you talk to someone face-to-face, your morals and what you think is different to when you are just talking to someone behind a keyboard."

Some students appeared to be able to reflect critically on the influence of anonymity, lessened socio-emotional cues, distance and instrumentality on moral reasoning, with respect to its effect on integrity, authenticity, honesty and accountability. In the section on the influence of ICTs on authenticity some students could understand that ICTs can influence the creation of false self-representations of themselves online.

Some moral psychologists have suggested that applying moral values to identify moral issues relies on self-awareness and self-evaluation of one's values and reasoning, and an awareness of the influence of one's actions on others (Barque-Duran, Pothos, Yearsley, & Hampton, 2016; Flores & James, 2013; Kerta, Uza, & Gecu, 2012; Schalkwijk et al., 2016). Some students expressed an awareness of the moral values they held and could, at some level, apply these to make moral judgements about their own behaviours.

Justifying Moral Judgements

Justifying moral judgements relies on: a) self-awareness and self-evaluation of one's own values and behaviours; b) an understanding of the influence of one's values on moral reasoning and behaviour; and c) an evaluation of alternative moral judgements. With respect to integrity, authenticity, accountability and honesty some students showed some level of self-awareness and self-evaluation of their own values while using ICTs and justified their moral judgments with respect to these values. However, students did not comment on their own evaluations of alternative moral judgements.

Determining Moral Action

"If someone is getting cyber bullied I'd tell the bully to back off." - Shouja

Determine moral actions involves identifying moral issues, critically assessing the detrimental influence of ICTs on authenticity and accountability, and determining actions that are morally justifiable. This requires individuals to: a) identify stakeholders; b) seek to understand the positions and needs of others; c) assess the consequences of actions on others; and d) determine the preferred outcome(s) for stakeholders.

Some students could do one or more of these. For example, with respect to justice, students claimed that they stood up for their peers who were cyberbullied, suggesting that they could understand the experiences of their peers, assess the consequences of actions and determine a moral action. With abilities and learning objectives outlined for moral reasoning, the next section describes how these can be fostered.

Fostering Values and Moral Reasoning

Fostering moral reasoning relies on: 1) the acquisition of moral values; 2) parental and adult guidance; 3) student-centred discussions (student voices); 4) learning from mistakes made while using ICTs; 5) positive peer pressure while using ICTs; 6) critical reflection about their experiences while using ICTs; and 7) school programs.

Parental Guidance

"I have the rule, if my mum would see it and be like, "Oh my God, it's terrible," I won't post." – Baba

"Parents inquiring into how the child is doing and guiding them is important." - Sparkly Eyes (a parent)

Parental involvement with adolescents promotes moral reasoning with respect to their uses of ICTs, which is a key factor in preventing cyberbullying (Buelga, Martínez-Ferrer, & Cava, 2017). Students, teachers and all parents suggested the importance of parental guidance in fostering values, moral reasoning and moral behaviour in the use of ICTs. For example, Sue (a parent) guided her daughter to think critically about what she posted on social media and noted that her daughter learnt from her advice and removed inappropriate postings: "The child took that down, so they made the decision, 'Well, you know what? You're probably right. It probably could be taken out of context, so I'll get rid of it.'"

Table 6.2 below summarised the shared values expressed by parents and their children with respect to the use of ICTs. This summary suggests the important influence parents have on their children's values. Some parents also suggested that parental supervision and clear expectations are important. During a teacher focus group, one teacher maintained that engaging year nine students in his classes by getting them to reflect on whether social media posts would pass the approval of a significant adult got students to think and was very effective. Robert (a teacher) noted, "That one worked well … that is the filter. That is the one that stops us from putting stupid things online."

Parents being connected to the social media accounts of their children is very important. However, in a year 12 focus group, students noted that parental guidance in their use was not as significant in year 12 as it was in year nine. The reason given was that their parents were no longer associated with their social media accounts as they were in year nine. Clairie, Baba and John (now Year 12 students) argued for the importance of adults engaging children earlier than year nine. This finding suggests the importance of early parental and school involvement.

Table 6.2 Shared values of parents and their children (C is child and P for parent)

	C	P	C	P	C	P	C	P	C	P
Values	Clairie	Sue	Louise	Spencer	Shouja	Sparkly Eyes	Baba	Aphro	Tim	Hodge
Integrity										
Honesty										
Trust										
Authenticity										
Accountability										
Empathy										
Responsibility										

Student Voices – Student-Centred Spaces

"I want to have a say." - Betty

Developing sensitivity to moral issues associated with the use of ICTs is more effective than seeking mere compliance to rules of conduct. Studies of ethical decision making while using ICTs indicate that personally held values play a greater role in determining behaviours than formal rules and informal codes that exist in organisational cultures in determining behaviours (Pierce & Henry, 1996; Volkman, 2015; Yoon, 2011).

Empowering individuals to have a voice is an important practice in seeking to foster values. Vickery (2012) describes this approach as *student-centred space*. Personal choice and decision-making are believed to support the development of self-identity in adolescents. Research on adolescents' conceptions of the teaching of values has shown that they are more likely to reject the teaching of values in schools by authorities who use top-down means of teaching. Adolescents prefer more autonomy-supportive forms of values teaching, such as open-ended discussions with opportunities for student reflection (Mcneil & Helwig, 2015). The students I engage with are generally enthusiastic about wanting to share their experiences with ICTs.

Some students suggested that fostering moral reasoning could be best achieved by providing young people with opportunities to think through their own values and choices, and have a voice in the values parents and teachers consider important for their uses of ICTs. Tyrone indicated, "Instead of just saying you should be doing this."

Marcus (a teacher) suggested:

> Ownership of online choices needs to be based on relatable norms, to have any impact. I include some norms below that my Self-Discovery class thought were important to

keep in mind. They felt self-regulation was the best option, discussing these options for some time and being genuine in this discussion. Would it stop poor choices? They felt it might, but circumstances can change as emotions can get in the way. The norms were: Ask, "would I say this face-to-face, to my grandmother? A teacher? Police?" Opt out of chat that is heading towards bullying. Think before posting, "How will this be received?"

Learning from Mistakes

"A lot of people will go back to what they've said on Facebook … and say 'Why was I was such an idiot?'" - Tyrone

Some computer ethicists suggest that challenging young people's moral reasoning with regard to their own behaviours and perspective-taking are recommended as a means of fostering morality in the use of ICTs (Lau & Yuen, 2014; Volkman, 2015). Cybernetics involves in part the ability to make ethical judgements in particular contexts and self-correct in the face of new information and one's mistakes. While using ICTs, young people are confronted by their own unethical behaviours and that of others, hence, moral learning can occur through mistakes made, as indicated by Tyrone.

Positive Peer Pressure

Relationships in peer groups play a role in fostering morality. For example, Tim said that honesty is fostered through what others see their peers doing online. He said, "If you're honest, you might be able to inform people to be more honest". Sue (a parent) suggested that "it can also be peer pressure associated with the use of technology. I think that there can be really good values coming out of it."

Taught to Reason Critically and Ethically

Ess (2002) argued that in the computer age, individuals need to think critically about their own values and those of others. Young people's actions that involve confronting problems in the world, making sense of them and making choices play a role in fostering morality. Some students' moral identity was fostered in the context their experiences while using ICTs. For example, with respect to integrity, accountability, altruism and inauthenticity some students could critically reflect about their experiences and reported having moral expectations of themselves. Providing young people with opportunities to discuss the moral expectations they have of themselves while using ICTs may be a method to foster moral reasoning and to construct their moral identity. Some students said that they needed to be taught how to reason critically with regard to the online content, without specifying what this meant. Through engagement, commitment and reflection, humans can transform their technological practices.

Derrick, a media studies teacher, said that critical thinking could be achieved in classroom discussion on the positive or negative effects of social media and new technologies, and through the use of film by identifying the moral reasoning, emotions and behaviours of the film characters. Robert (a teacher) said that he would also use this approach to explore internet scams: "You could work on the basis of what's being compromised by looking at their values." He also suggested that emphasising the detrimental effects of unethical behaviour and using ethical dilemmas that relate to students' life experiences could be beneficial for fostering values and moral reasoning.

School Programs - Best Practice

Students suggested that school programs played a role in fostering authenticity. Louise said, "That [the school program] got me to realise that I don't want to change who I am depending on whether I'm around my family or around my friends". While discussing school-based educational programs with year 12 students, Baba and Clairie questioned the effectiveness of these programs, noting that in their current format they were not engaging. Baba maintained, "They are irrelevant, they are not in touch with what kids are actually doing online. They can't give accurate warnings because they (teachers and parents) don't know about the social media they are using." This suggests that education provided by adults must be relevant, timely and age appropriate to be effective. This also suggests that "Digital Student Ambassadors" may be well placed to contribute to school programs.

Cyber safety is the main educational approach currently being used in schools. One concern about cyber safety programs is what Gotterbarn (1992) calls 'pop computer ethics'. This teaching approach seeks to sensitise individuals to ethical issues by drawing on horror stories promulgated through the use of ICTs. However, focusing on risks and cautionary tales may leave students with the impression that computer related ethical issues are promulgated by a few individuals, are difficult to solve, or are largely irrelevant to them personally. This approach places the emphasis on the unethical, rather than a proactive approach by encouraging students to consider their own moral values and behaviours. The suggested pedagogical approach when using the Digital Moral Framework is that learning can occur when individuals are empowered to change their values and behaviours through reflecting and applying these to their own and their peers' uses of ICTs.

Teachers made four recommendations with respect to school-based programs. First, fostering values should begin earlier than year nine. Second, students should have opportunities to reflect on their values before they start using ICTs. Third, young people needed to learn empathy through human interactions first, away from the screen, by seeing empathy being modelled around them. This suggests the importance of primary level values education that schools implement. Fourth, although parents may have values, they may not necessarily have the knowledge and the skills to teach moral reasoning with respect to the use of ICTs. The implication of this observation is the need to provide parents with support to acquire the skills to foster moral reasoning.

Table 6.3 below, summarises the moral reasoning abilities that are important. Additionally, the abilities and learning objectives associated with integrity, authenticity and accountability, the influences in the students' lives that foster values, and the teaching and learning methods used to foster moral reasoning are summarised.

Table 6.3 Moral Reasoning in the Use of ICTs, and Teaching and Learning

| Values: |
| Integrity, Authenticity and Accountability |

Abilities and Learning Objectives

Identify moral issues and make moral judgements based on these values.

Have moral expectations of oneself based on these values, which relies on self-awareness and self-evaluation of one's own values and behaviours.
For example, critically reflecting if one is being true to one's values and consistent with one's self-presentations while using ICTs.

Justify moral judgements based on these values, which relies on: a) self-awareness and self-evaluation of one's own values and behaviours, b) an understanding of the influence of one's values on moral reasoning and behaviour and c) an evaluation of alternative moral judgements.

Determine moral actions based on these values. This involves identifying moral issues, critically assessing the detrimental influence of ICTs on authenticity and accountability, and determining actions that are morally justifiable. This requires individuals to: a) identify stakeholders, b) seek to understand the positions and needs of others, c) assess the consequences of actions on others, d) determine the preferred outcome(s) for stakeholders.

Influences on Fostering Values and Moral Reasoning
The acquisition of moral values
Parental and adult guidance. Parents need to be associated with social media accounts when children are young.
Student-centred discussions (student voices)
Learning from past mistakes
Positive peer pressure
Critical reflection about their experiences while using ICTs
School programs
Teaching and Learning Methods Student-centred dialogue such as soliciting the views of students about significant values and the role peers played in the practices. Linking discussions about values to the lives of young people. Using ethical dilemmas related to students' life experiences. Use the 'see, think and wonder' approach. Critical evaluations of values and behaviours that mediated the uses of ICTs. Learning from mistakes Start lessons by defining terms, the reason for the presentation and the goals of the lesson. Explore integrity, heart and character in the use of ICTs using Y charts 'sounds like, feels like and looks like'.

CHAPTER SEVEN

Heart – Values and Moral Emotions in the Digital World

This section discusses the role of moral emotion in relation to the values of empathy and conscience, the abilities associated with these values, and how these values and abilities can be fostered.

Empathy in the Digital World

Empathy is both a cognitive and emotional reaction of an individual to the observed experiences of another. The abilities associated with empathy are: 1) cognitive empathy - reasoning about one's own emotions and another person's experiences and emotions; and 2) empathic concern is defined as concern for others' negative experiences, which can lead to behaving morally (caring for others). Emotional empathy involves feeling the same emotion as another person and feeling compassion for another. I do not cover emotional empathy since it was not possible to determine if students experienced this.

Reasoning About Our Own Emotions

"It was not fair to blame others without putting yourself in other people's shoes."

- A student

Empathy influences a person's understanding of the nature of caring. Evaluating and managing one's emotions well is considered important for moral behaviour (Goleman, 2004; Malti & Latzko, 2012). Being aware of one's emotions and managing them well can play a role in considering the situation of another while using ICTs. Recent findings on cyberbullying show that emotion regulation is a potential target for intervention among young people who have higher levels of cyberbullying (Wang et al., 2017).

While using ICTs some students appeared to understand their own emotional reactions and discern the morally relevant factors of a situation, such as not blaming others without knowing their circumstances. Empathy is associated with more lenient moral judgments of others, while blaming others is associated with moral disengagement and may override empathic responses in the use of ICTs (Runions & Bak, 2015). With respect to emotion regulation, some students considered it unfair to blame others without "putting yourself in other people's shoes", which suggests that they tried to discern the morally relevant factors of a situation and sought to adjust their moral judgments of others accordingly. This behaviour is an indication that empathy and/or justice played a role in evaluating and managing their own emotion (blame) and judgement of others.

Reasoning About Others' Experiences and Emotions

The ability to consider a situation from another's point of view is one prerequisite for moral reasoning and moral behaviour (Davis et al., 2010). *Cognitive empathy* also involves reasoning with regard to another person's experiences and emotions. The abilities associated with cognitive empathy are: a) the ability to take another person's perspective, such as understanding the experiences and emotions of others - recognising that moral transgressions have a negative influence on others; b) discerning the relevant moral factors of a situation; and c) understanding that moral transgressions have negative consequences on others.

One study found that youth cyber-bystanders of cyberbullying were able to perceive others' emotional states (Spears et al., 2013), which suggests that cognitive empathy is possible in the context of the use of ICTs by young people. Some students could, at some level, consider the situations of others, understand what others were experiencing and feeling (upset and depressed), and understand that moral transgressions (cyberbullying) had negative consequences on others. However, these was no indication that this understanding led to feeling empathy for their peers. Some parents and teachers maintained that year nine students do not typically have highly developed levels of emotional empathy.

Behaving Morally - Looking After Others

"There's always good things going on Facebook ... Someone might be having a hard day and they'll post something ... saying like, I'm there for you." - Tim

Empathy and conscience help adolescents to anticipate the outcomes of socio-moral events and adjust their moral action tendencies accordingly. Empathy supports motivation for actions and is associated with prosocial behaviour in children (Barque-Duran et al., 2016; Malti & Latzko, 2012). Tim and Louise spoke about the empathic concern, which lead them and some of their peers to look after their friends when they were upset and comforting them when they were cyberbullied. They also appeared to be able to anticipate negative social outcomes for their peers (depression and emotional upset) and identify positive social outcomes when they and their peers intervened to help them.

Some students maintained that empathic concern displayed by young people was beneficial to the emotional wellbeing of their peers in need. The classroom and student interview data were rich with examples of self-reported empathic and caring behaviours while using social media. Some students appeared to consider empathy while using social media to be beneficial to the wellbeing of their peers who were depressed. For example, Louise said that showing empathy and care "gives them a reason to stick around ... So it's pretty important."

Empathy also acts as a protective factor that promotes young people's psychosocial wellbeing. Three students maintained that the practice of empathy is beneficial to their peers in need. Dee, an IT teacher, also supported this view, stating, "You'll have issues where somebody has been picked on, on *Facebook* and some students jump on and support that person."

Conscience in the Digital World

"A lot of people will go back to what they've said on *Facebook* ... and say 'Why was I was such an idiot?'" Tyrone

The abilities associated with conscientiousness are: 1) listening to our 'intuition of rightness and wrongness' (the voice of our conscience before a behaviour) and remorse - (the voice of our conscience felt after a wrong behaviour); 2) evaluating the negative consequences of our actions on others (Learning from mistakes); 3) taking the perspective of others; 4) acting morally based on one's conscience; and 5) repairing what we did wrong.

Remorse

Conscience relies on self-conscious emotions such as remorse, which plays a role in self-evaluation and moral judgement. Experiencing remorse indicates an awareness of the consequences of one's inappropriate actions on others.

Conscience influences behaviour because it acts as an 'intuition of rightness and wrongness' - the voice of the conscience before a behaviour or as a remorse - the voice of the conscience felt after an inappropriate behaviour. If an individual has internalised values and does not act accordingly, they experience an internal sanction in the form of a negative self-evaluation, feelings of remorse or a bad conscience (Allison & Bussey, 2017; Blasch & Ohndorf, 2015).

Some students spoke about the remorse they and their peers felt about inappropriate actions while using social media, which suggests not only that they could, at some level, evaluate the negative consequences of their actions on others, but also that they had some ability to take the perspective of others. Additionally, this suggests that they understood the emotion they felt (remorse).

Acting Morally Based on one's Conscience

Some students also spoke about feeling a desire (conscience or a sense of justice) to stand up for others who were being bullied. Shouja indicated, "I'm not exactly sure what the word I'm looking for is, but just like the feeling of just going on with it and pumped up to go for it and that you'd feel better after doing it." Dee (a teacher) maintained that the conscience was important because it "sets the foundation of your reasoning. I think children that have a bit more of a moral compass would genuinely behave more morally online."

In Table 6.1, conscientiousness is ranked twelfth by students. However, it is worth noting that conscientiousness is also considered to be a sense of holding oneself accountable. In the interview extracts on integrity and accountability, Shouja, Betty, Clairie and Louise appeared to express their sense of holding themselves accountable for their own practices while using ICTs, suggesting that this sense of responsibility may be linked to conscience. The findings on remorse are important because some students appeared to have developed internalised values and experienced internal sanctions (remorse) when they acted in ways that they felt contradicted their values.

Fostering Empathy

This section explores the views of students, parents and teachers in relation to fostering cognitive empathy (reasoning about one's own emotions and another person's experiences) and empathic concern and caring for others, and fostering conscience.

Fostering cognitive empathy and empathy concern relies on: 1) the acquisition of moral values and reasoning with regard to these values; 2) emotional self-awareness and emotion differentiation in moral judgements; 3) learning to consider the perspective and needs of others; 4) taking an active interest in the concerns of others - behaving morally; and 5) empathy shown by significant adults and people around us.

However, both parents and teachers argued that fostering empathy in this age group (14 and 15 year olds) was a challenge. Robert (teacher) noted, "This is the ultimate educational challenge, whether you have an impact on their feelings about the issues, so that they will become active thinkers and doers in that regard."

Acquiring Values

The acquisition of values is critical when seeking to fostering moral emotions, this is because the values held by individuals bring out self-evaluative emotions (empathy and remorse) (Krettenauer & Johnston, 2011).

Fostering Emotional Self-Awareness and Differentiation

Moral emotions influence reasoning. The empathy and remorse experienced while using ICTs influenced some students' understanding of the nature of caring and responsibility. Empathy and conscience builds on emotional self-awareness and self-assessment. Some students were aware of their own emotions (empathy and remorse), were aware that it was not fair to blame others without knowing their situation, suggesting that they could differentiate between fairness/empathy and blame. With respect to remorse and self-awareness, some students reported feeling remorse for inappropriate actions and learning from their mistakes. It is likely that the emotional self-awareness and self-evaluation, the experience of empathy and conscience reported by some students while using ICTs may have been a factor in fostering these moral emotions.

Considering the Perspective and Needs of Others

Moral emotions develop in children when they learn to distinguish between their own personal perspectives and those of others, and become aware that moral transgressions have negative consequences on others. The self-reported empathetic behaviours displayed by some students on social media in response to the perceived distress of their peers, suggests that some were aware of the needs of others. Encouraging such an awareness may be a factor in fostering empathy. Hodge (a parent) maintained that empathetic behaviours online, such as "picking up on people that are having some difficulty out there" and "putting yourself in another person's shoes," fosters empathy in young people. It is possible that empathy and remorse may have been reinforced through events occurring in ICT environments. Encouraging such reflection may be a factor in fostering moral emotions.

Some literature in moral psychology suggests that empathy can be taught effectively through school-based programs, where students learn to distinguish between the perspectives of the self and others (Noddings, 2010), and that moral transgressions have a negative impact on others (Malti & Latzko, 2012). Teachers recommended two teaching and learning methods that could be used to foster consideration of the perspective of others. First, linking lessons to students' own experiences, and second, focusing classroom discussion on the positive or negative effects of ICTs on others. During one classroom presentation, the teacher began the lesson by showing students pictures of young people who were affected by cyberbullying. This activity appeared to elicit empathic concern in students. Narratives and appeals to emotions have the biggest impact on moral change as children's socio-moral sensitivity can be fostered by discussing conflict situations and the emotions they invoked in students as victim, perpetrator, bystander and observer (Malti & Latzko, 2012).

During the 2017 teacher focus group, Robert noted that during his year nine personal discovery classes, students shared about the cyberbullying they participated in and were the victims of. He maintained that some learnt empathy through this and even stood up for others. Robert noted, "To build morality they must have seen or understood the consequences of actions."

Empathetic Behaviours - Taking an Active Interest in the Concerns of Others

Empathy is linked to an active desire to alleviate another's suffering. Some students appeared to take an active interest in the suffering of their peers while using ICTs. Some students appeared to suggest that their own empathetic behaviours fostered empathy, because of the emotional reward this brought, namely, feeling good about one's empathetic behaviours online.

Clairie (a student) stated that empathetic behaviours "makes me, in turn, feel nice that my comments have been appreciated and have had a positive outcome on the recipient" and another student said it feels "like you make a difference to someone." Sparkly Eyes (a parent) said that empathy could be nurtured by parents showing interest in their children; "rather than getting home, doing dinner and, "Yeah, done your homework? Yeah? Go to bed." However, fostering empathy was argued by parents to be a challenging task for this age group.

Fostering Conscience

Fostering conscience also relies on: 1) the acquisition of moral values and reasoning with regard to these values; 2) emotional self-awareness and emotion differentiation in moral judgements; and 3) learning to consider the perspective and needs of others.

Acquiring Values

One study concluded that reducing the reasoning processes that allow adolescents to avoid moral-emotional reactions such as remorse is one important factor in fostering the moral development of young people. As long as harmful effects of behaviours are ignored or distorted, there is little reason for moral self-sanction to be activated (Paciello et al., 2017).

Emotional Self-Awareness and Considering the Perspective of others

Remorse allow individuals to learn from moral mistakes. Discussing conflict situations and the emotions they invoke in students can help to foster children's socio-moral sensitivity. Some students indicated that emotional learning occurred from past mistakes made while using ICTs. It is likely that the emotional self-awareness and self-assessment reported by some students with respect to empathy and remorse may have been a factor in fostering these moral emotions. Robert (a teacher) maintained that students' experience of remorse for actions on social media should be included in the teaching of values, "because this side of technology has allowed them to do it, so I can see how it would feel. I think it would be very interesting to keep that in mind when we do the lessons."

Table 7.1 below summarises the abilities and learning objectives associated with empathy and remorse, the influences in the students' lives that foster these values, and the teaching and learning methods used to foster moral emotion.

Table 7.1 Moral Emotion, and Teaching and Learning

Values: Cognitive Empathy, Empathic Concern and Conscience
Abilities and Learning Objectives
Reasoning about one's own emotions. Evaluating and managing emotions helps us understand emotions felt and how this influences behaviour. Managing the impulse to blame others by understanding how blame influences on our judgements of others and adjust our judgements accordingly.
Reasoning about another person's experiences and emotions involves: a) the ability to take another person's perspective, such as understanding the experiences and emotions of others; b) discerning the relevant moral factors of a situation, such as evaluating the consequences of one's behaviours on others; and c) understanding that moral transgressions have negative consequences on others - taking the perspective of others.
Empathic concern involves concern for others' negative experiences, which can lead to behaving morally (caring for and looking after others).
1) Listening to our intuition of rightness and wrongness (the voice of our conscience before a behaviour) and remorse - (the voice of our conscience felt after a wrong behaviour).
2) Evaluating the negative consequences of our actions on others (Learning from mistakes); 3) taking the perspective of others; 4) acting morally based on one's conscience; and 5) repairing what we did wrong.
Experiencing remorse helps: Evaluate the consequences of one's behaviours on others. Influences one's ability to take the perspective of others.

Empathic concern involves concern for others' negative experiences, which can lead to behaving morally (caring for and looking after others).

Conscience involves:
1) Listening to our intuition of rightness and wrongness (the voice of our conscience before a behaviour) and remorse - (the voice of our conscience felt after a wrong behaviour).
2) Evaluating the negative consequences of our actions on others (Learning from mistakes); 3) taking the perspective of others; 4) acting morally based on one's conscience; and 5) repairing what we did wrong.

Experiencing remorse helps:
> Evaluate the consequences of one's behaviours on others.
>Influences one's ability to take the perspective of others.

Fostering cognitive empathy and empathic concern relies on:

1) the acquisition of moral values and reasoning with regard to these values; 2) emotional self-awareness and emotion differentiation in moral judgements; 3) learning to consider the perspective and needs of others and recognising that moral transgressions have a negative influence on others; 4) taking an active interest in the concerns of others - behaving morally; and 5) empathy shown by significant adults and people around us.

Fostering Conscience relies on:
1) the acquisition of moral values and reasoning with regard to these values; 2) emotional self-awareness and emotion differentiation in moral judgements; and 3) learning to consider the perspective and needs of others.

Teaching and Learning Methods
1. Teaching moral values.

2. Discussions around student's own experiences and considering the perspective and experiences of others while using ICTs. Being aware of one's emotions can play a role in considering the situation of another while using ICTs.

3. Narratives and discussions that appeals to emotions.

4. Self-awareness and self-assessment of one's values, emotions and behaviours -
Learning from one's mistakes.

5. Encouraging students to take an active interest in the concerns of others.

CHAPTER EIGHT

Character – Values and Moral Behaviours in the Digital World

Moral character and behaviours require moral self-management such as the self-regulation of impulses and moral behaviours towards others, such as justice. With respect to adolescent morality, character is defined as the psychological and social skills required for moral behaviour (Lau & Yuen, 2014). This is significant as some research indicates that good self-management (responsibility, self-control and accountability) plays an important role in moral reasoning and moral behaviour (Baggio & Beldarrain, 2011), and studies have consistently shown that moral self-regulation shapes moral behaviour (Barque-Duran et al., 2016; Berkowitz et al., 2002).

Morality is intrapersonal because morality involves us defining who we are and how we should be like (values and identity). It is also interpersonal (how we behave towards others). Both these dimensions are critical for the moral use of ICTs. In the DMF, moral self-management - the intrapersonal dimension is based on the values of self-control and responsibility, while moral behaviour towards others – the interpersonal dimension is based on the values of altruism, justice and respect.

Moral Self-Management

Moral self-management while using ICTs relies on: 1) acquiring values and being self-aware and making moral decisions based on self-control and responsibility; 2) having moral expectations of oneself; and 3) behaving morally based on self-control and responsibility. Managing our disputes, postings, the spreading and accessing of inappropriate content, refraining from anti-social behaviours, managing emotions and risky behaviours, and controlling the information individuals reveal about themselves involve self-control and responsibility. The students were the most concerned about the lack of responsibility because of the problems associated with the list above.

Self-control and ICTs

"If you are on technology you can go out of your limits (in the level of inappropriate social media postings) and think that was too far, but you can't control it because of someone else doing it to you as well." - Betty

Even if young people are able to identify moral concerns, they do not necessarily act morally; therefore, this is where moral self-management becomes important. This view was shared by some teachers. For example, Robert noted the lack of moral self-management in year nine students:

> I tried to understand why we see so much cyberbullying. Kids that know it's wrong to do it, but still participate in bullying. We are now reviewing the schools cyberbullying policy and we are trying to figure out how we are going to deal with this in the future.

One definition of moral self-management is an individual's set of psychological characteristics that affect that person's ability to function morally and regulate behaviours. Self-control plays a role in underpinning moral behaviour, such as managing inappropriate emotions, desires and actions in favour of appropriate ones, refraining from anti-social behaviours, and managing emotions and risky behaviours while using ICTs (Houck et al., 2014).

The use of ICTs is associated with more hurried responses and emotional reactions. This may be an important factor in how individuals use ICTs. Some students considered self-control important in managing emotional reactions while using ICTs. For example, they reported that self-control is important in order to not hurt others and to manage anti-social behaviours, such as inappropriate social media posting and how they respond to the postings of others. Shouja said that some of her peers "get carried away" and post things "they probably didn't want to imply." Louise also talked about some of her peers airing disputes on social media.

Self-Control and Privacy

Self-control also plays a role in controlling the information individuals reveal about themselves and others while using ICTs. Shouja and Tim said that self-control was important to manage how young people portray themselves on social media.

"There are things on the web that aren't meant to be viewed by younger people. There is no stopping them." Tim

Self-control also plays a role in managing the content young people accessed. Some parents also commented that self-control is needed to control the amount of time young people spend using ICTs.

Self-control and responsibility was considered important by some students for moral self-management and moral actions towards others, while a lack of self-control and responsibility was suggested to adversely affect the moral behaviour of students. Self-control is ranked fourth with respect to the 12 moral values studied (see Table 6.1), while a lack of self-control is ranked seventh with respect to the 14 moral concerns identified by students (see the list of Technologically Mediated Moral Issues in chapter three).

Acquiring values, being self-aware, making moral decisions and having moral expectations of oneself

Some students could identify some moral issues associated with self-control, noting that it was important for respecting others, self-respect and treating others justly, which suggests that some students were aware of their own need for self-control when making moral decisions, had expectations of themselves based on self-control (in order to not hurt others and oneself), and determining a moral action.

However, there are no data to suggest that self-control actually underpinned their behaviours.

Responsibility and ICTs

"Those who take pride in who they are, get along with people and try hard to do everything, they will be more respectful and more cautious on social media." - Louise

Many students commented on the importance of responsibility while using ICTs. For example, Tim maintained that "you might really want to say something there, but you know if you do, it won't be the right thing…" The following extracts could also have been used as examples of justice, but in this instance, they also apply to social responsibility. Shouja noted, "If someone is getting cyber bullied I'd tell the … bully to back off," while Baba said, "I just like to be responsible and make sure everything is going okay." Tim suggested that some of his peers also felt responsible for those who were targets of derogatory postings on social media; "I have seen people standing up for others… and … try to help…"

Parents ranked responsibility in ninth position and teachers ranked it in eighth position in relation to the 12 values; however, responsibility is ranked first by students. The disparity between the views of adults and students in this regard, is likely that adults do not necessarily understand the experience of young people when it comes to a lack of responsibility shown by their peers while using ICTs. The data suggest that several students could make moral decisions and appeared to have moral expectations of themselves based on their own sense of responsibility and social responsibility for others, while in some instances they reported that they behaved accordingly.

Their own sense of responsibility, self-control and accountability are all ranked in the top six values, suggesting the importance these students place on managing themselves well.

Behaving Morally Towards Others

Behaving morally towards others while using ICTs relies on: 1) acquiring values; 2) analysing moral issues and determining moral actions associated with the use of ICTs based on altruism, justice and respect, and making moral decisions; 3) having moral expectations of oneself; and 4) behaving morally based on altruism, justice and respect.

Altruism and ICTs

"People are really kind in general, and they'll just offer themselves as best they can." - Tim

Many students noted that altruism is important in the use of ICTs. Some students reported on the altruistic behaviours they considered important, such as "caring" and "performing random acts of kindness", "doing good for others", "treating others well" and "being kind."

Altruism is important because it influences moral behaviour and fosters the wellbeing of others. For some students, looking after their peers when they are upset or getting cyberbullied was also important. Tim held the view that "caring for others" and, going "out on a limb for them" were important behaviour for him, while Louise talked about guiding her peers in relation to their inappropriate uses of ICTs, "because you don't want to get them in trouble." Altruism can be motivated by the good feelings that come from giving (self-reward), self-esteem or conforming to one's moral values. Some students had moral expectations of themselves with respect to altruism and some appeared to be motivated by the reward that came with being altruistic. In Table 6.1, altruism is in second position. These findings suggest that altruism is a value that is important for moral behaviour.

Justice and ICTs

Justice is considered to play an important role in analysing moral issues associated with the use of ICTs (Bynum, 2008; Floridi, 1999; Yoon, 2011), and behaving morally (Grappi, Romani, & Bagozzi, 2013). Findings suggest that some students could make moral decisions, had moral expectations of themselves based on justice, and in some instances, reported acting in situations calling for justice. In Table 6.1, justice is ranked in third position by students.

Year 12 Students on Altruism and Justice

"In year nine it (approval of one's peers) was more important, but we are a lot more mature now and I don't really care for approval." – Baba in year 12

Some year 12 students argued that altruism and justice is not generally practised by their cohort, yet, John one of the year 12 students stated that, "if one of our peers crosses the line, people will say something." One year 12 student suggested that the importance of peer approval and a reluctance to stand up to others online was greater in year nine, suggesting that this may have influenced the prevalence of online altruism by this cohort.

Standing Up to Injustice

"It's incredibly hard for them to stand up and have the courage at this age (year nine)." - Dee (a teacher)

"If someone is getting cyber bullied I'd tell the ... bully to back off." – Shouja (a student)

Research suggests that adolescents consider justice important for themselves and others. However, despite their potential to reduce the influence of cyberbullying, most bystanders do not intervene in witnessed incidents. Yet, those with stronger beliefs that cyberbullying is wrong should feel more compelled to intervene (Allison & Bussey, 2017). Students commented on the importance of justice, particularly when it came to cyberbullying. Some said that they believed in treating others the way they wanted to be treated and made efforts to not put others down when online. Students also reported their own pursuit of justice in situations where their peers were being cyberbullied. For example, they reported that they stood up for others online, indicating that justice played a role in the moral behaviour of these young people. Tyrone reported intervening in a bullying situation, saying, "You don't really need to write that" and recommended to his peers "to stand up" and "speak out" in cyberbullying situations.

Year 12 students did not appear to use social media for bullying as much as in year nine. This may be because of the understanding that year 12 students have about the public nature of social media postings. For this reason, year 12 students suggested some of their peers used private messaging services to avoid public disapproval. A wider audience may mean that young adults are conscious not to interact in an overly emotional way through social media because of the more intense surveillance of friends' activities (Niland, Lyons, Goodwin, & Hutton, 2015).

Most parents also considered justice to be important. Spencer expressed the same sentiments as her daughter Louise, with respect to pursuing justice online, noting, "She does not like the bullying thing. She's usually the first one to say 'don't pick on people'," However, Stuart (a teacher) suggested that students do not regularly stand up for their peers, stating, "You get the exceptions where all stand up and try to make a difference, but in general they want to be accepted" by their peers.

Respect and ICTs

"Respect others and they'll respect you … don't disrespect people, for everyone to see." – Tim

"If you're respectful, you're respectful of who you are as a person. You respect who others are." - Louise

Most students considered respect to be an important behaviour for both themselves, and their peers. Adolescents desire privacy while using ICTs (Boyd, 2014). Some parents and students noted that young people needed to have self-respect, particularly with regard to respecting the privacy of their bodies, by not posting explicit photos of themselves on social media.

Student, parents and teachers also shared their concern for respecting the privacy of others while using ICTs. Woody (a teacher) suggested, "I think those students who struggle with respect for themselves don't have as much control over what they are doing on their iPads, as opposed to those students who do have respect". For teachers, respect for cultural diversity and women was also important. In Table 6.1, students ranked respect in seventh position, which was the same weighting as empathy. Parents ranked respect in fifth position, while teachers ranked it in second position. Based on these findings, respect can be considered one of the key values. Several students could make moral decisions, had moral expectations of themselves based on respect and in some instances reported having self-respect and respecting others. Responsibility, altruism and justice are values associated with social responsibility for others. Students considered these values as the most important in the use of ICTs.

The following section discusses how moral behaviour might be fostered.

Fostering Self-Control and Responsibility, and Altruism, Justice and Respect

The findings suggest that fostering moral self-management (self-control and responsibility) and moral behaviours in relation to others (altruism, justice and respect) while using ICTs relies, in part, on: 1) the acquisition of moral values; 2) analysing moral issues associated with ICTs; 3) parental guidance; 4) positive peer pressure; 5) self-reflection about one's behaviours, and self-evaluation of how one can improve; 6) behaving morally; and 7) school programs. In my study, the greatest influences on fostering moral self-management and moral behaviour are parents, peers and self-reflection.

Acquiring Moral Values and Analysing Moral Issues

Acquiring moral values is important for moral behaviour since in adolescents, internalised moral values have been shown to be associated with prosocial engagement. Additionally, changing peer culture requires convincing young people to see themselves as part of a community and to accept responsibility for each other (Berkowitz et al., 2002). Altruism, justice and respect allow individuals to acknowledge their responsibility with regard to their decisions and behaviours, and how these affect others.

Some students reflected on the need for altruism, justice and respect; therefore, encouraging such reflections that relate to students' life experiences may be important in fostering a sense of responsibility for others. A study of cyberbullying recommended that teaching moral reasoning may help foster a sense of responsibility for others (Spears et al., 2013). Conversely, disengagement with moral reasoning directly predicted cyberbullying intentions of adolescents (Lazuras et al., 2013).

Some computer ethicists have maintained that identifying moral problems relating to the use of ICTs based on moral values can be used to foster a sense of moral responsibility (Gotterbarn, 1992; Liua & Yanga, 2012). Some students could identify moral issues with regard to altruism, justice, respect, which appeared to be linked to their desire to be caring, fair and respectful. Some students also appeared to be able to critically analyse their own behaviours and the behaviours of their peers with respect to a lack of self-control and responsibility while using ICTs. This suggests that self-reflection and self-evaluation, and critical analysis can play a role in fostering self-control and responsibility.

Parental Guidance

Parental involvement and connection with adolescents promotes moral reasoning and behaviour (Padilla-Walker & Christensen, 2011), while a lack of parental involvement in the use of ICTs by their children and inappropriate peer values are related to more risky behaviours while using ICTs (Livingstone & Smith, 2014). Additionally, family relationships characterised by a positive family climate and open and empathic parent and child communication act as protective factors against children becoming cyberbullies and coping with being cyberbullied. By contrast, cyberbullies more commonly have dysfunctional family relationships characterised by poor emotional attachment to their parents (Buelga et al., 2017).

Three students noted that their parents' values and guidance were an important influence on their moral behaviours while using ICTs. Four parents and two teachers also said that values education coming from parents plays a role in fostering moral behaviour in the use of ICTs by young people. For example, Sparkly Eyes (a parent) maintained that the guidance she provides is effective because her child consulted with her: "She would bring that to me to say, 'I don't think it's right, what they're talking about this girl'. We brought up our kids with good values, which I think follows through to the internet." Sue (a parent) also maintained that values education and communication "helped out our children to be able to use things in a correct fashion."

Parental supervision and imposing consequences for misbehaviours were also proposed by some parents and teachers as a means to foster values and moral behaviour. For example, Aphro (a parent) noted, "parents need to read what the children are writing (on social media). If they think what they're doing is inappropriate, they need to educate their children on what they can and can't do." As a parent, Sue suggested setting limits on the usage of ICTs as a means of fostering self-control. She said that if there were no limits set, "they would probably just go on them 24/7, if they could." Two parents maintained that teaching children not to take things for granted also fosters responsibility. Sue held the view that "in our family, I think the fact is that it's not to be taken for granted. … it's something that you earn the right to be able to use and use it in a responsible way."

Positive Peer Pressure

Our peers "would give us a hard time when we are not respectful." – A student

Peer pressure also plays a role in the behaviour of teenagers. In previous student data on altruism, justice and respect, peer pressure appeared to foster these values in students. Tyrone described an incident on *Facebook* where some in his cohort were being ranked as the "top ten worst". "That's when a lot of people went, that's just too far. ... you don't really need to write that." Betty and Tim suggested that respecting others fosters this behaviour in their peers. Tim maintained, "just respect others and they'll respect you." Paul (a parent) suggested that peers can have a positive influence on the behaviours of young people. He provided an example of peers influencing the decision of a student that was ready to leave school but continued because of the encouragement that came from his friends on social media. One teacher also recommended mobilising peer pressure to foster moral values and behaviours. Dee referred to this as "positive-wise".

> If a peer calls them out on their behaviour, they will take that on board almost immediately ... In some ways, I would like to see this being taught by another student to a bunch of younger students. I think their voice would be a lot more powerful than our voices". "I think peer pressure would change culture. So, the more educated the students become, the more pressure there is to behave in a certain way.

Self-reflection and self-evaluation

Self-reflection of one's behaviours and self-evaluation of how one can improve, influences how we treat others. These abilities were seen by some students and teachers as a means of fostering respect and justice. Louise (a student) suggested that knowing herself and others helped her respect others. Louise also suggested that fostering a sense of pride in oneself, getting along with others and being respectful could foster responsibility in the use of ICTs. Woody (a teacher) suggested that self-reflection supports self-control: "I guess it comes back to that issue of self-control and being aware of how actions can impact on yourself and other people. So, I guess it's that awareness of self." Self-control involves goal-directed behaviour in the face of important, competing inputs and actions. The implication is that self-awareness of one's goals and values may be a factor in fostering self-control.

Emphasising the value of justice in students' everyday experience is suggested as an important teaching practice (Liua & Yanga, 2012; Pugh & Phillips, 2011). Therefore, student discussions that centre on evaluating their own behaviours and the behaviours of their peers could be used to foster moral self-management, and altruism and justice. An inquiry-based teaching approach that encourages reflections about the harmful effects of misbehaviours towards others and defining the problems associated with misbehaviours are considered effective teaching methods because self-reflections influence how we treat others (Barque-Duran et al., 2016; Malti & Latzko, 2012; Watson, 2014).

Behaving Morally

"There is always people convincing people of good ideas." - Tim

Moral behaviours allow moral values to be internalised and engaging in moral behaviours increases satisfaction and self-esteem (Allison & Bussey, 2017; Berkowitz et al., 2002; Krettenauer & Johnston, 2011). Research suggests that many examples of adolescent social activism and prosocial behaviour involving the use of ICTs can be found (Vickery, 2012). The use of ICTs can facilitate civic engagement and promote social responsibility. In my study there were examples of empathy for others, and standing up for justice. The data on altruism, justice, respect and responsibility suggests that personal and social responsibility were considered the most significant values in the use of ICTs by the students. Based on these findings, encouraging young people to practise altruism, justice, respect and responsibility in their online communities could be an effective means of fostering moral behaviour.

The promotion of good causes through ICTs was seen by some participants as a means of fostering altruism and moral behaviour. Dee (a teacher) provided an example of social activism initiated by students at the school in the form of a website set up to discuss issues of youth suicide. Some research suggests that altruism is motivated by the good feelings that come from giving (self-reward), guilt reduction, self-esteem or conforming to one's moral values (Blasch & Ohndorf, 2015). Some students indicated that they felt good about doing good things online. This suggests that this may have reinforced altruism.

Young people engaging in prosocial experiences with peers can enhance altruistic attitudes that can lead to these becoming part of their moral identity (Paciello et al., 2017). It is not enough just to lecture about values; young people need to practise them so that they can build essential emotional and social skills. For example, community service can be an effective way of developing civic commitment in young people, as it promotes doing, rather than merely studying values. There is a current trend for secondary schools to implement mandatory community service programs. The secondary school in which this study took place also had such a program, called 'The Common Good'. These prosocial programs are seen as beneficial for fostering moral reasoning and moral behaviour. Recent research has found that adolescents are not simply self-focused but they also balance and coordinate considerations of autonomy and community in their reasoning about community service programs

(Mcneil & Helwig, 2015). Therefore, community service programs supplemented with classroom discussion and personal reflection are considered to be a means to enhance the positive outcomes of service programs.

School Based Programs

Some students suggested that school-based programs could play a role in fostering moral reasoning and behaviour. Tim suggested, "I think people, when they're young, when they're just getting to the stage where they're starting to use technology we need to teach them self-control … I just don't think it's taught." Three parents also suggested that school-based values education could augment what parents do in the home.

Table 8.1 Moral Behaviour, and Teaching and Learning

Table 8.1 summarises the abilities and learning objectives associated with self-control, responsibility, altruism, justice and respect, the influences in the students' lives that foster these values, and the teaching and learning methods used to foster moral behaviour.

Values: Self-control and Responsibility
Abilities and Learning Objectives Moral self-management while using ICTs relies on: 1) acquiring values and being self-aware and making moral decisions based on self-control and responsibility; 2) having moral expectations of oneself and 3) behaving morally based on self-control and responsibility. Managing emotional reactions with respect to not hurting others, how you respond to others, airing disputes, posting and spreading inappropriate content about yourself and others, accessing inappropriate content, refraining from anti-social behaviours, managing emotions and risky behaviours, and controlling how much time is spent using ICTs.
Influences on Fostering Values and Self-control and Responsibility Fostering moral self-management (self-control and responsibility) and moral behaviours in relation to others (altruism, justice and respect) while using ICTs relies on: 1) the acquisition of moral values; 2) analysing moral issues associated with ICTs; 3) parental guidance; 4) positive peer pressure; 5) self-reflection about one's behaviours, and self-evaluation of how one can improve; 6) behaving morally; and 7) school programs.

Values: Altruism, Justice and Respect
Abilities and Learning Objectives   Behaving morally towards others while using ICTs relies on: 1) acquiring values; 2) analysing moral issues and determining moral actions associated with the use of ICTs based on altruism, justice and respect and making moral decisions; 3) having moral expectations of oneself; and 4) behaving morally based on altruism, justice and respect, namely: Having self-respect   Respecting the privacy of others   Caring for peers in need.   Standing up to bullies and reporting them.   Guiding others well   Behaving justly.   Showing and earning respect.   Respecting cultural diversity and gender.   Respecting one's privacy and that of others.
Fostering moral behaviours in relation to others (altruism, justice and respect) while using ICTs relies on: 1) the acquisition of moral values; 2) analysing moral issues associated with ICTs; 3) parental guidance; 4) positive peer pressure; 5) self-reflection about one's behaviours, and self-evaluation of how one can improve; 6) behaving morally; and 7) school programs.

Teaching and Learning Methods
1) Structured reflection/ self-Assessment about:

Students' life experiences while using ICTs and identify moral problems relating to the use of ICTs

The critical evaluation of one's own uses of ICTs.

2) Parental guidance
Family relationships characterised by a positive family climate and open and empathic parent and child communication.

3) Parental supervision and imposing consequences for misbehaviours

4) Positive Peer Pressure

5) Behaving morally
Social activism and prosocial behaviour involving the use of ICTs

6) School programs

Conclusion

With respect to policy and practice, this book provides further understanding of adolescents' moral development by considering the relationship between morality, ICTs and teaching and learning. The Digital Moral Framework (DMF) suggests that the moral domains play an important role in the moral use of ICTs by secondary school students. In my study, students showed some abilities with respect to having moral agency in all three moral domains. The two key abilities that stand out are self-reflection of one's values and behaviours and critical analysis of the values and practices that mediate the use of ICTs. The DMF and the CVS model provide teaching and learning tools that can be used to stimulate conversations with young people about the moral self-reflection and the moral critical analysis they need to have with respect to their uses of ICTs. This book also suggests learning objectives, influences, and teaching and learning methods that parents and teachers can use in their conversations with their children. Learning can occur when young people have a voice in the values that are important for their uses of ICTs, engage with content that they consider to be relevant for them and can critically reflect on the values that mediate the use of ICTs and apply moral values to their uses of ICTs.

References

Allison, K. R., & Bussey, K. (2017). Individual and collective moral influences on intervention in cyberbullying. *Computers in Human Behavior, 74*, 7-15.

Arıcak, O. T., Dündar, Ş., & Saldaña, M. (2015). Mediating effect of self-acceptance between values and offline/online identity expressions among college students. *Computers in Human Behavior, 49*, 362-374.

Baggio, B., & Beldarrain, Y. (2011). *Anonymity and Learning in Digitally Mediated Communications: Authenticity and Trust in Cyber Education.* Hershey, PA: IGI Global.

Barlett, C. P. (2017). From theory to practice: Cyberbullying theory and its application to intervention. *Computers in Human Behavior, 72*, 269-275.

Barque-Duran, A., Pothos, E. M., Hampton, J. A., & Yearsley, J. M. (2017). Contemporary morality: Moral judgments in digital contexts. *Computers in Human Behavior, 75*, 184-193.

Barque-Duran, A., Pothos, E. M., Yearsley, J. M., & Hampton, J. A. (2016). Patterns and evolution of moral behaviour: moral dynamics in everyday life. *Thinking & Reasoning, 22*(1), 31-56.

Bartlett, W., & Prica, I. (2017). Interdependence between core and peripheries of the European economy: secular stagnation and growth in the Western Balkans. *The European Journal of Comparative Economics, 14*(1).

Bats, J., Valkenburg, R., & Verbeek, P.-P. (2013). *Mediating Technology: How ICT Influences the Morality of the Digital Generation*. Paper presented at the International Confrence on Engineering Design, Seoul, Korea.

Baumeister, R., & Liua, D. (2016). Social networking online and personality of self-worth: A meta-analysis. *Journal of Research in Personality, 64,* 79-89.

Baumgartner, S. E., Sumter, S. R., Peter, J., & Valkenburg, P. M. (2015). Sexual self-presentation on social network sites; Who does it and how is it perceived? *Computers in Human Behavior, 50,* 91-100.

Berkowitz, M. W., Colby, A., Kristol, I., Power, C., Schwartz, A. J., Sherman, N., . . . Walker, L. (2002). *Bringing in a New Era in Character Education.* Stanford: Hoover Institution Press.

Berkowitz, M. W., & Grych, J. H. (1998). Fostering Goodness: Teaching Parents to Facilitate Children's Moral Development. Retrieved from http://tigger.uic.edu/~lnucci/MoralEd/articles/berkowitzfostering.html

Blasch, J., & Ohndorf, M. (2015). Altruism, moral norms and social approval: Joint determinants of individual offset behavior. *Ecological Economics, 116,* 251-260.

Blau, I., & Eshet-Alkalai, Y. (2017). The ethical dissonance in digital and non-digital learning environments: Does technology promotes cheating among middle school students? *Computers in Human Behavior, 73,* 629-637.

Boyd, D. (2014). *It's Complicated: The Social Lives of Networked Teens.* New Haven and London: Yale University Press.

Buckingham, D. (2008). *Youth, identity, and digital media.* Cambridge, Mass. : MIT Press

Buelga, S., Martínez-Ferrer, B., & Cava, M.-J. (2017). Differences in family climate and family communication among cyberbullies, cybervictims, and cyber bullyevictims in adolescents. *Computers in Human Behavior, 76*, 164-173.

Bynum, T. W. (2008). Computer and Information Ethics. In *The Stanford Encyclopedia of Philosophy*: Stanford University.

Cameron, J. D. D., & Payne, K. (2013). Morality in high definition: Emotion differentiation calibrates the influence of incidental disgust on moral judgments. *Journal of Experimental Social Psychology, 49*(4), 719-725.

Casey, B. J. (2015). Beyond Simple Models of Self-Control to Circuit-Based Accounts of Adolescent Behavior. *Annual Review of Psychology, 66*, 295-319.

Cho, V. (2017). A study of negative emotional disclosure behavior in social network media: Will an unexpected negative event and personality matter? *Computers in Human Behavior, 73*, 172-180.

Christie, C., & Dill, E. (2016). Evaluating peers in cyberspace: The impact of anonymity. *Computers in Human Behavior, 55*(292-298).

Colby, A., & Damon, W. (2015). *The Power of Ideals The Real Story of Moral Choice*. New York, NY: Oxford University Press.

Davis, K., Gardner, H., Rundle, M., Francis, J. M., Flores, A., Pettingill, L., & James, C. (2010). Young People, Ethics, and the New Digital Media. *Contemporary Readings in Law and Social Justice, II*(2), 215-284.

Ent, M. R., Baumeister, R. F., & Tice, D. M. (2015). Trait self-control and the avoidance of temptation. *Personality and Individual Differences, 74*(February), 12-15.

Ess, C. (2002). Computer Mediated Colonisation, the Renaissance, and Educational Imperatives for an Intercultural Global Village. *Ethics and Information Technology, 4*(1), 11-22.

Ess, C., & Thorseth, M. (2010). *Global information and computer ethics.* Cambridge, UK Cambridge University Press

Flores, A., & James, C. (2013). Morality and ethics behind the screen: Young people's perspectives on digital life. *New Media Society, 15*(6), 834-852.

Floridi, L. (1999). Information Ethics: On the philosophical Foundations of Computer Ethics. *Ethics and Information Technology, 1*(1), 33-52.

Giner-Sorolla, R. (2012). *Judging Passions Moral Emotions in Others and Groups* London and New York: Psychology Press.

Goleman, D. (2004). *Emotional Intelligence and Working With Emotional Intelligence.* London: Bloomsbury Publishing.

Gotterbarn, D. (1992). The Use and Abuse of Computer Ethics. *Journal of Systems and Software, 17*(1), 75-80.

Grappi, S., Romani, S., & Bagozzi, R. (2013). Consumer response to corporate irresponsible behavior: Moral emotions and virtues. *Journal of Business Research, 66*(10), 1814-1821.

Greenfield, K. S. P. (2008). Online Communication and Adolescent Relationships. *The Future of Children, 18*(1), 119-146.

Heesen, J. (2012). *Computer and Information Ethics.* London: Elsevier Inc.

Heirman, W., & Walrave, M. (2008). Assessing Concerns and Issues about the Mediation of Technology in Cyberbullying. *Cyberpsychology: Journal of Psychosocial Research on Cyberspace,, 2*(2).

Heylighen, F., Joslyn, C., & Turchin, V. (1999). What are Cybernetics and Systems Science? Retrieved from http://cleamc11.vub.ac.be/REFERPCP.html

Houck, C. D., Barker, D., Rizzo, C., Hancock, E., Norton, A., & Larry K. Brown. (2014). Sexting and Sexual Behavior in At-Risk Adolescents. *Pediatrics, 133*(2), 276–282.

Juthberg, C., & Sundin, K. (2010). Registered nurses' and nurse assistants' lived experience of troubled conscience in their work in elderly care—A phenomenological hermeneutic study. *International Journal of Nursing Studies, 47*(1), 20–29.

Kerta, S. B., Uza, C., & Gecu, Z. (2012). Scenarios for computer ethics education. *Procedia - Social and Behavioral Sciences, 46*, 2706 - 2710

Krettenauer, T., & Johnston, M. (2011). Moral self and moral emotion expectancies as predictors of anti- and prosocial behaviour in adolescence: A case for mediation? *European Journal of Development Psychology, 8*(2), 228-243.

Krettenauer, T., & Malti, T. (2013). The Relation of Moral Emotion Attributions to Prosocial and Antisocial Behavior: A Meta-Analysis. *Child Development, 84*(2), 397-412.

Lau, W. W. F., & Yuen, A. H. K. (2014). Internet ethics of adolescents: Understanding demographic differences. *Computers & Education, 72*, 378–385.

Lazuras, L., Barkoukis, V., Ourda, D., & Tsorbatzoudis, H. (2013). A process model of cyberbullying in adolescence. *Computers in Human Behavior, 29*(3), 881–887.

Lim, J. S., Nicholson, J., Yang, S.-U., & Kim, H.-K. (2015). Online authenticity, popularity, and the "Real Me" in a microblogging environment. *Computers in Human Behavior, 52*, 132-143.

Liua, C. J., & Yanga, S. C. (2012). Applying the Practical Inquiry Model to investigate the quality of students' online discourse in an information ethics course based on Bloom's teaching goal and Bird's 3C model. *Computers & Education, 59*(2), 466-480.

Livingstone, S., & Smith, P. K. (2014). Annual Research Review: Harms experienced by child users of online and mobile technologies: the nature, prevalence and management of sexual and aggressive risks in the digital age. *Journal of Child Psychology and Psychiatry, 55*(6).

Malti, T., & Latzko, B. (2012). Moral Emotions. In *Encyclopedia of Human Behavior (Second Edition)* (pp. 644-649): 2 Elsevier Inc.

Mcneil, J., & Helwig, C. C. (2015). Balancing Social Responsibility and Personal Autonomy: Adolescents' Reasoning About Community Service Programs. *The Journal of Genetic Psychology, 176*(6), 349-368.

Mercier, H. (2011). What good is moral reasoning? *Mind & Society, 10*(2), 131-148.

Niland, P., Lyons, A. C., Goodwin, I., & Hutton, F. (2015). Friendship Work on Facebook: Young Adults' Understandings and Practices of Friendship. *Journal of Community & Applied Social Psychology, 25*, 123-137.

Nissenbaum, H. (1994). Computing and Accountability. *Communications of the ACM, 37*(1), 72-79.

Noddings, N. (2010). Moral education and caring. *Theory and Research in Education, 8*(2), 145–151.

Paciello, M., Muratori, P., Ruglioni, L., Milone, A., Buonanno, C., Capo, R., . . . Barcaccia, B. (2017). Personal Values and Moral Disengagement Promote Aggressive and Rule-Breaking Behaviours in Adolescents With Disruptive Behaviour Disorders. *International Journal of Offender Therapy and Comparative Criminology, 61*(1), 46-63.

Padilla-Walker, L. M., & Christensen, K. J. (2011). Empathy and Self-Regulation as Mediators between Parenting and Adolescents' Prosocial Behavior toward Strangers, Friends, and Family. *Journal of Research on Adolescence, 21*(3), 545-551.

Perren, S., & Gutzwiller-Helfenfinger, E. (2012). Cyberbullying and traditional bullying in adolescence: Differential roles of moral disengagement, moral emotions, and moral values. *EUROPEAN JOURNAL OF DEVELOPMENTAL PSYCHOLOGY, 9*(2), 195-209.

Pierce, M. A., & Henry, J. W. (1996). Computer ethics: The role of personal, informal, and formal codes. *Journal of Business Ethics, 15*(4), 425-437.

Price, M., & Dalgleish, J. (2010). Cyberbullying - Experiences, impacts and coping strategies as described by Australian young people. *Youth Studies Australia, 29*(2), 51-59.

Pugh, K. J., & Phillips, M. M. (2011). Helping Students Develop an Appreciation for School Content. *Theory Into Practice, 50*, 285-292.

Runions, K. C., & Bak, M. (2015). Online Moral Disengagement, Cyberbullying, and Cyber-Aggression. *Cyberpsychology, Behaviour and Social Networking, 18*(7).

Schalkwijk, F., Stams, G. J., Stegge, H., Dekker, J., & Peen, J. (2016). The Conscience as a Regulatory Function: Empathy, Shame, Pride, Guilt, and Moral Orientation in Delinquent Adolescents. *International*

Journal of Offender Therapy and Comparative Criminology, 60(6), 675–693.

Sicart, M. (2009). *The ethics of computer games*. Cambridge, Mass.: MIT Press.

Sikka, T. (2012). A critical theory of technology applied to the public discussion of geoengineering. *Technology in Society, 34*(2), 109-117.

Spears, B., Price, D., Green, D., Scrimgeour, M., Barnes, A., Geer, R., & Johnson, B. (2013). A Qualitative Exploration of Cyber-Bystanders and Moral Engagement. *Australian Journal of Guidance and Counselling*, 1-17.

Valkenburg, P. M., Koutamanis, M., & Vossen, H. G. M. (2017). The concurrent and longitudinal relationships between adolescents' use of social network sites and their social self-esteem. *Computers in Human Behavior, 76*, 35-41.

Vickery, J. R. (2012). *Worth the Risk: The Role of Regulations and Norms in Shaping Teens' Digital Media Practices*. (Doctor of Philosophy), The University of Texas, Austin.

Volkman, R. (2015). Computer ethics beyond mere compliance. *Journal of Information, Communication and Ethics in Society, 13*(3/4), 176-189.

Wang, X., Yang, L., Yang, J., Wang, P., & Le, L. (2017). Trait anger and cyberbullying among young adults: A moderated mediation model of moral disengagement and moral identity. *Computers in Human Behavior, 73*, 519-526.

Watson, M. (2014). Developmental Dicipline and Moral Education. In L. P. Nucci, D. Narváez, & T. Krettenauer (Eds.), *Handbook of moral and character education*. New York, NY Routledge.

Wee, J., Jang, S., Lee, J., & Jang, W. (2017). The influence of depression and personality on social networking. *Computers in Human Behavior, 74,* 45-52.

Wong, E. Y. W. (1995). How should we teach computer ethic? A short study done in Hong Kong. *Computers Education, 25*(4), 179-191.

Yoon, C. (2011). Ethical decision-making in the Internet context: Development and test of an initial model based on moral philosophy. *Computers in Human Behavior, 27*(6), 2401-2409.

www.ingramcontent.com/pod-product-compliance
Lightning Source LLC
Chambersburg PA
CBHW082120070326
40690CB00049B/4020